Moving On

Bryan Paul Lai

Moving On
Copyright © 2019 Bryan Paul Lai

All rights reserved. No part of this publication may be reproduced, distributed, or transmitted in any form or by any means, including photocopying, recording, or other electronic or mechanical methods, without the prior written permission of the author, except in the case of brief quotations embodied in critical reviews and certain other non-commercial uses permitted by copyright law.

THE JOURNEY CONTINUES....

SABAH

Leave nothing but Footprints

Take nothing but Memories

ACKNOWLEDGMENT

I would like to express my appreciation and profound thanks to the following inner circle of associates: Tan Sri Simon Sipaun (Former Sabah State Secretary), Datuk Wilfred Lingham (Former Permanent Secretary to Local Government and the president of Sabah Government Pensioner Association), Datuk Vincent Pung (CEO of Sabah Credit Cooperation), Mr. Chia See Boon (the chairman of the Tawau historical society), Mr. Joseph Jominol (chairman of PPKS Penampang), Mr. Wong Vui Yin (the director of State Public Library Kota Kinabalu), Mr. Carl Traulson (the son of Mr. Horace Traulson, now living in USA), Mr. Eddy Sophian Pulle of Sawit Kinabalu Group, Encik Hamit Harun (the former deputy assistant administrative director of the Chief Minister Department and the secretary general of Sabah Government Pensioner Association), Mr. David Ho (former auditor of JKM, and the Treasurer of Sabah Pensioner Association), the Late Mr. Ricatea Azcona, Mr. Patrick Chin, Mr. Lawrence Missi of Penampang and all my unwavering friends who gave me the incentive of my story to enable me to finalize this third book entitled "Moving On". Last but not least to my wife Koh Lee Kyaw and my children for their analytical remarks and support.

My First Inspiration

My First Book "The Joy Of Life" Was The Catalyst That Inspired Me To Write My Second Book. Being A Novice, The Journey Had Not Been Easy. The Final Push To Present The Final Product To The Publisher Had Been Slow, Due To Glitches. In Spite Of This, I Kept Pushing On, Knowing That Dreams Could Only Be Achieved Through Hard Work

And Perseverance. I Need To Fulfil This Quest That I Had Since Young. I Need To Prove To Myself And My Family That Nothing Is Impossible To Achieve Once You Set Your Mind To It.

After My Maiden Book Was Published And Made Available To The Public, The Positive Responses Had Been Exciting. This Inspired Me And Invigorated Me To Continue With My Second Book.

The Second Book, "A Glance Of Tawau In The Sixties" Took Me Two Years To Complete. Extra Photos Were Added To Enhance The Story. After All, "A Picture Is Worth A Thousand Words".

With This Book, My Third One, I Write With The Intention To Conclude The Final Episode Of The Story, As I Move On Towards The Reflection And Experiences Of My Life.

EPISODE 1

The Closing Scene of my vocation

I had lived through the British rule and survived the World War II as an infant. I was there to observe the formation of Malaysia, and the endured the turbulent times during the Indonesian Malaysian confrontation. I continued moving on with life during the period of uncertainty as the political arena of the nation moved on uncharted territories.

I have been living in Tawau for more than fifty years, seeing it growing from a small sleepy town to the busy municipality as it is now.

After being trained as a teacher, I was first posted in a school in Semporna. After a while, I was able to serve in Tawau. Teaching was a profession that I had chosen with no regrets.

Throughout my teaching career, I have the wonderful opportunity to get to know many teachers from all around our country, including those from West Malaysia. The West Malaysians were posted all the way here to complement the teaching fraternity in Sabah as there were not enough of our trained teachers to accommodate all the schools in our state. As a result, I am proud and honored to have made many close friends from all across Malaysia.

After serving for twenty-nine long years, retirement has come knocking on the door, calling me to exit with dignity, promising me a life free from encumbrances and a life tied down by duty. Throughout my service as an educator in the government service, there is a limitation to indulge in the things that I wanted to do. As a retiree, I will be free to follow the path of my interest.

The school that I left after my retirement in 1998

On my last day of being an educator, the full impact of this day suddenly hit me as I was clearing up all my personal belongings in my office. The last steps I took walking out of my office was a painful and heart-breaking experience, especially, as I began to leave the school compound. My beloved staff of teachers and non-teaching staff were gathered along the walkway with all my pupils to bid me farewell. It was hard to hold back my tears as I saw some of them wiping away tears and some were even openly bawling.

No matter how heartbreaking leaving the community you have been together for years, retiring is part and parcel of life. We need to move on and enjoy the last remaining years to continue living a life creating a different set of memories.

I will be forever grateful as those years of service had given me ample experiences that made me into the person I am today - self-reliant and prepared to face the uncertainties of life. During my younger days, the school and church had been the only sanctuary I knew. I had spent more of my time in school than the comfort of my home. Now, I intend to increase the time spent with my family and friends.

A NEW ROLE

During the earlier days of my retirement, my contribution to the church was considered as 'minimal'. However, two years later, Rev Father Tung the rector of Holy Trinity Church Tawau approached me. He asked me to assist him to manage the three Catholic Schools Board. The former chairman Datuk James Pang had decided to call it a day due to time constraint.

I was hesitant to accept the post, as I knew that I could not provide the necessary service as an ordinary retiree.

After much coaxing from Rev Father Tung and a promise to only let me hold the post momentary, I accepted with trepidation. I served for two years and decided to hand over the post as promised.

Rev Father Tung

Regrettably, Rev Father Tung was transferred by then, and Rev. Father Cosmas had taken over as the rector. Rev Father Cosmas asked me to continue holding the post until he managed to get a replacement. With that, I ended up serving for two more years before I voluntarily resigned for good.

With extra time to indulge in, I was then able to spend more quality time with my families and friends. Meanwhile, in order to spend my time positively and with zero stress, I indulged more time in hobbies. I started planting some fruit and cocoa trees in my small 'kebun'.

Spending quality time with the grandchildren
in my sanctuary at Sin On Tiku Tawau

My sanctuary, near the Tawau Tanjung Forest
Reserve 12 kilometers from town.

    I call this small 'kebun' my getaway, a sanctuary and a place to relax myself physically and mentally. Located around 12 kilometers away from the hustle and bustle of town life, it is located at the fringe of a forest reserve called the Tanjung Forest reserve.

The Tanjung Forest Reserve 12 kilometers from Tawau Town

The Tanjung Forest Reserve still abounds with tall trees that had escaped the wrath of the timber merchants in the sixties. It is an area that has a unique attraction. At that time, the bird and wild animals roamed free in that area. However, in 1980, a section of the surrounding forest was alienated to the Tawau Golf Club to build the second golf course in Tawau. This development, while good for the Tawau community, has somewhat affected the flora and fauna of the forest.

Aside from the Tanjung Forest Reserve is another forest reserve and water catchment area called the Tawau Hills Park. It is located north of Tawau at Sime Darby estate. The Park had been upgraded and beautified by the Government to promote that area for recreational purposes.

In addition to the beauty of the park and the waterfalls, stands the tallest tropical tree in the world.

The Tawau Hills Park. By courtesy of Mr. James Ku Hien Leong

Moving On

Mr. James Ku Hien Leong looks like a dwarf standing in front of the tree.

EPISODE 2

The gloomy cloud

Every beginning has an end. "From dust, you come unto dust you shall return", death has always been human's final destiny.

My sister in law was in her prime of life when she discovered she had some health problem. She did her very best to find a cure but failed. After several years of suffering, she succumbed to the disease and passed away peacefully. A few years later my father who had been ill succumbed to his disease and finally passed away in the year 2001.

The family in the solemn mood

Before the dark cloud of sorrow could drift away, my sister and two brothers were called by the Lord. The moment when every ordeal came in sequence. My mother was overcome by these unexpected events. Her strong conviction in her faith and a firm believer in God kept her going.

Several months passed, and the grief-stricken events steadily forgotten by the passing of time. We continued to provide financial, compassion and moral support.

Our Sandakan trip

In the year 2006, I received an invitation from the Sandakan Municipal Council to attend the Anzac event in Sandakan. An event to honor those killed during the second world war of 1941-1945. I told my mom Gabriella that we would be bringing her to Sandakan to attend the Anzac Memorial Ceremony on 15 August 2006.

The Sandakan Memorial Site

In the past, my father was invited, but due to work, he could not attend. As the eldest son in the family, I accepted the invitation. She was very happy and delighted when I broke the news to her. I was happy to see a smile on her face.

Gabriela's trip to Sandakan had a profound meaning to her. It's the town where she was born, grew up and started a family during her teen years. She grew up in Kampong Gulam. At ten years of age, Gabriella lost her mother who died at age thirty-six.

Her last visit to the kampong was in 1978 when many of the sisters were still around. Now, many of them had either gone to the Lord or had gone overseas. This would be her first visit after many years. A homecoming to her place of birth in 1926.

Sandakan in 1944

The scheduled day came, and after making sure that the vehicle was fit for the road, we drove all the way to Sandakan. I was accompanied by my wife Lilian Koh Lee Kyaw, my mother Gabriela Remedia Lobos and my niece Natasha. We stayed at a local hotel close to the memorial site. That evening we were invited to attend a dinner banquet at the official resident of Datuk Yeo Boon Hai, the president of Sandakan Municipal Council.

At the residence dinner party in Sandakan

Dinner at the Sandakan Municipal's President Resident 2006

The next early morning we arrived in time to witness the roll call. The ceremony began with the sound of the bugle, speeches by prominent guest and lying of the wreath. I was then invited to address the crowd.

The author Bryan Paul Lai at the Anzac Memorial Service held in Sandakan in the year 2006

The host and Guest at the ceremony in
Sandakan Anzac Memorial Service

The memorial service ended at around ten in the morning and breakfast was served. The next day, a lady by the name of Doreen Hurst from Australia, met my mom Gabriela Remedia Lobos at the Sabah Hotel. They had an hour of casual conversation pertaining to mom's experience during the Second World War. Doreen was on the verge of finalizing her book entitled "Sandakan 1941-1945". The book portrayed the sacrifice and adversity of the local inhabitants during the war. It was based on the local resistance giving help to the prisoner of war in Sandakan. She promised to donate part of her proceed to the people of Sabah when the book reached the market for sale.

I thanked her for her gratitude and generous proposition. Meanwhile, I kept my finger cross, until the day she fulfilled her generous contribution came into my hand.

We drove back to Tawau after the event was over. The trip had made some consolation to my mother to see the name of her husband being immortalized at the memorial plaque. Mom, as usual, kept herself busy trying to bury the hatches of the past.

EPISODE 3

A short trip to Kota Kinabalu

I visited Kota Kinabalu several times during the year to attend the Sabah Government Pensioners meeting. During the visit, my children gave out feelers to their mother, indicating their desire for us to move out from Tawau and make Kota Kinabalu our new home. A signal of their concern for our well-being and welfare.

The surprise request put us in a very difficult predicament. It never crossed our mind or the idea of moving out from Tawau town. We have been living since young. Tawau was then a simple town with only several rows of shops. We studied, worked, got married and earned our living as teachers for the last thirty years. My wife Lilian Koh was born in Tawau and most of her siblings and relatives were in Tawau.

Most of my ex-students and many friends were all in the hamlet of Tawau. The only place I felt comfortable and could move about with my eyes closed.

Our physical attachment was great. To move out, might cause mental and social anxiety.

But, after the death of my father and sibling, the situation had changed. We took the children's request seriously. Finally, in the year 2009, we decided to move out from our comfort zone.

Before such a move could be made, several issues needed to be finalized. Such as our house and the small piece of land. Several months later, we sold the house and got my brother in law Ahmad Yusuf to manage the Kebun.

I always believe that life is made of time frames. Every frame has its purpose. We need to move on and out of the box. We cannot bind and chain ourselves to a limited environment to our usual routine of life. As Jean Piaget, the renowned psychologist once said: "Intelligence is the ability to adapt to the new environment."

Tawau town in the 1950s

A Mystical Call?

Besides my children's request, I had an unexplainable feeling that kept urging me to move to Kota Kinabalu. That persistent voice inside my head was getting stronger with each passing day, and it was as if the universe conspired to give us the confidence to finally move to the capital of Sabah. I teasingly told my family that it was the spiritual call of my ancestors to return to Jesselton – what Kota Kinabalu was called during the times of my ancestors.

My grandfather, Austin Lai Man, worked with the British North Borneo Chartered Company. He was a station master at the railway department. He spent his younger days at Papar town and later moved to Jesselton. Unfortunately, he died in 1943 during the Japanese occupation, the year I was born. With that I was deprived of the privileged to know my grandfather.

The type of train my grandfather used to work with in Jesselton. Courtesy of Datuk Wilfred Lingham

Jesselton in the early years of North Borneo

Jesselton town (Api Api) in North Borneo. Courtesy of Evelyn Lim

The Jesselton Civil hospital.

Besides my grandfather, my father used to spend a significant amount of his working life in Jesselton. My father Peter Raymond Lai worked at the Civil Hospital.

In 1947, the Medical Department of the colony of North Borneo produced the first magazine called *SIMPALILI The Spectral Tarsier*. The magazine was forwarded by His Excellency Mr. E.F. Twining, C. M. G., M.B.E. Governor and Commander- in- Chief of the colony of North Borneo.

In the magazine, Peter, my father wrote part of it on Sea Sickness, Ben Stephens who was the Laboratory Assistant, wrote on Urine Testing and its significance, Mr. H. G. Keith on village medicine in North Borneo and Doctor K.H. Blaauw a medical officer in Tawau on a case of intestinal obstruction caused by lumbricoides.

During my father's tenure of duty, the hospital was in a dire state of disarray. There was no equipment to provide proper medical care to the patients. The doctor-in-charge was Doctor Clarke who tried his utmost best to manage the hospital as best as he could.

Proper housing accommodation were a hard find in those days, so Peter was given a depleted house close to the hospital compound. When Peter first moved in, he discovered that there were still human remains carelessly thrown under the house. With the help of the hospital attendant, Peter gave the deceased a decent burial.

Mr. Pang Vui Chau, a dresser during the Japanese occupation, gave a vivid recollection of how the hospital managed to cope during the Japanese occupation.

Mr. Pang was at the epic centre of the Japanese occupier. He had witnessed how the war had caused so much destruction to the town.

Mr. Pang Vui Chau was lucky to survive, despite the hardship he encountered during the occupation by the Japanese imperial army. An episode of bitter experience that continued to disturb him emotionally even in his dreams after the war.

According to him, during the first year of the war, the hospital was still able to survive on the massive stock pile of medicine by The Chartered Company. Twelve months later, during the Japanese occupation, the supplies dwindled to a dire state. They had no other alternative but to beg for medical supplies from the rubber estate company to supplement their requirement.

It was later that Japanese medicine was brought in, much to the relief of the hospital management. In August 1942, a Japanese health officer Doctor Ota was assigned to the hospital to take over the rein of the chief medical officer. However, he confined his treatment only to the Japanese soldiers. Doctor J.C.T. Tragarthen, the current district surgeon, was assigned to treat the locals. In the last few months of 1942, Doctor P.T. Lian and Doctor Lopez were roped in to help Doctor Tragarthen.

The doctors and staff were faced with extra duties when 700 British and Australian prisoners of war were brought in. The prisoners were assigned to help to build the Tanjung Aru runway. Many of the prisoners succumbed to all types of diseases, due to lack of proper food and rest. Through the kindness and compassion of Doctor Ota, they were admitted into the civil hospital and given proper medical treatment. Doctor and Mrs. MacArthur, who were prisoners themselves, were immediately released from internment, and given the permission to work at the hospital. In April 1943 Doctor Ota was replaced by Doctor Hironika. Doctor Koya, also a Japanese doctor, was the Dental surgeon.

The Japanese kampitai, through their local informant, received words that the Kota Kinabalu guerrillas planned to attack the Japanese garrison.

With no reason given, both Doctor Tragarthen and Doctor MacArthur and their families were detained. They were sent to Kuching Prisoner of War Camp. The local resistance from Sandakan who were also arrested was among those sent to the same prison. My father Peter was also among them.

A few days later the uprising began on 9 October, the guerrilla's fighters were down with so many wounded.

Several of the hospital dressers - Wong Boon Chua, Peter Lee, Ethelbert Dominic and Pang Vui Chau were abducted by the guerrillas and were brought to their headquarters at Menggatal to treat the casualties.

Mr. Peter Lee was released and told to return to the hospital to hoard some medicine and returned to the camp. However, he failed to return due to roadblocks manned by the Japanese. Peter Lee, unable to fulfil the demand by the guerrillas, continued to work in the hospital till the end of the war. The military took over most of the hospital wards to treat their wounded soldiers.

In 1944, the civil hospital had no other alternative but to transfer whole stock and barrel to Beaufort. Mr. Philip Lee with a few more junior dressers then established their dispensary in Jesselton town with Doctor Yoshimura in charge.

The dispensary was bombed in February 1945. Whatever medicine and equipment that were salvaged were placed in a kampong town. The dispensary was then relocated to Inanan town due to the extensive bombing by the allied forces.

As a result, there were no medical supplies to treat the sick. To survive, many resorted to traditional remedy. Herbs were used to treat all sorts of sicknesses and the kampong folks used a special prayer called 'SaiKung' to treat the sick.

The situation in Jesselton and the surrounding areas were in a dire state. There were no medical supplies to treat the wounded and the town was completely destroyed due to the bombing of the allied warplanes.

The doctors and staff who had sworn to treat the wounded and heal the sick, could only watch helplessly as the death toll increased by the hour. The never-ending groans of pain and pleadings of help would only stop when the victims closed their eyes forever. Mr. Pang Vui Chau could never erase the terrifying ordeal of the war from his memory until the day he died.

Moving On

Jesselton in 1940

EPISODE 4

Bon Voyage

Tawau in the 1960

Finally, in the year 2010, Lilian and I heartbreakingly bid farewell to our beloved town Tawau.

I was at the airport waiting to board the flight. My mind began to travel back to the past, reminiscing in a sentimental mood, all the sweet and happy days living in Tawau town.

Moving On

My mind flashbacked to the very first day that I put my footprint in this town in 1949, similar to Astronaut Armstrong's first step onto the lunar surface.

However, instead of a spaceship, I came by steamship from Jesselton, passing through Kudat, Sandakan, Lahad Datu and then finally arriving to Tawau.

The Tawau Wharf

Arriving by steamship in Tawau, the first thing that greeted us was the sight of a fragile looking wooden wharf that looked as if it was dancing to the tune of the tide.

The old Tawau jetty in 1940

A rail track could be seen all the way to the end of the jetty. We had to be careful as we disembarked from the ship. A narrow plank was placed hanging from the ship's deck onto the wharf. Ropes were tied on both sides to prevent us from slipping into the sea. The flimsily built wooden jetty swayed from the beating of the waves and the movements of the ship. Lose planks were everywhere, threatening to injure or trip any careless person.

My 'kampong' Tinagat

As I continued walking down memory lane, I recalled interesting stories related to me by an old man called Talip. His village was at Tinagat, Batu Payung, Tawau. Batu Payung means 'an umbrella made of stone'. There was an old legend passed on by the people of the village about what happened a hundred years ago.

A young warrior of the village went to the seashore to gather some wood on the beach. Out of the blue, he saw a beautiful maiden sitting on top of a huge stone. Enchanted by her beauty, he asked her to descend from the stone so he could get acquainted with her. She refused in spite of his pleas. Determined to speak to her, the young warrior took out his axe and proceeded to cut around the stone to bring it down. It took him a lot of time and effort, but he never gave up. Finally, as he was about to complete hacking the stone, the beautiful maiden had vanished, disappearing into thin air. He was divested and was literally madly in love that he killed himself with the same axe and died at the same spot. The stoned that was hacked resembled an umbrella, and that was how the name Batu Payung came about.

The day the Japanese landed in Tinagat

Another recollection, I had of Tinagat is about the day when the Japanese landed there. This story was told to me by an old friend named of Talip. I met him while he was helping dad to build his dream house by the shore.

Talip lived in a small village call Batu Payung. On that fateful day, as usual, he would be at the sea side collecting clams and setting up his net for the days catch. He was not aware that the world was on the brink of war. He tried to take a moment of cat nap, but could not due to the sand flies that bothered him endlessly.

Undeterred, he covered up his head with his sarong, only to find his net was moving in the water. He quickly went into the water to retrieve his catch. Suddenly, when he looked out into the horizon, he saw a fleet of boats coming on shore with fully armed people in uniforms.

Alarmed, he abandoned his net and ran up the slope and hid behind some bushes nearby. Along the road, he saw a government vehicle coming towards where the Japanese had landed.

Out came the Tawau British administrator Cole Adams and his assistant to meet them. The Japanese military immediately detained them instead. Cole Adams was completely surprised and shocked to receive such rude treatment from the Japanese soldiers.

Talip watched the whole incident in horror, and kept silence throughout. He dared not move nor make a sound. This would attract the Japanese attention and he might be shot. As soon as the Japanese soldiers left, he quickly retrieved his catch and went back to his village, informing them that the Japanese had landed.

After the war, Talip continued to live in the village at Batu Payung.

Soon after, my dad Peter bought a piece of land at Tinagat, situated at the seaside. A beautiful piece of property right at the edge of the seashore. It has a stunning view of the bay and Sebatik Island.

Talip was staying nearby, a walking distance from the land my dad had bought. Before the war, he worked as a building contractor and knew some construction experience. Dad took him in and both of them did the building work for six months. With Talip's help, dad managed to finish his dream house. Our Tinagat home was indeed an almost perfect place to live. The only problem was the lack of electricity and water supply at that time.

However, along the journey to our perfect home, lies a place that has a sinister past. Whenever my dad drove past this place, he would become somber and my mom would offer a silent prayer. We children would remain silent, feeling Goosebumps as we gazed out the car window. This place was known as the Massacre Hill. Until today, many villagers in Tinagat swore they could still hear the cries of the massacred when the nights are silent. The massacred were victims of the Japanese occupation during the Second World War.

EPISODE 5

Japanese Occupation

After arriving in Tawau, the Japanese took over the administration of the town without any resistance. The people were told that the Japanese were there to liberate them from the fangs of the colonial power. Life went on as usual and the people continued their daily chores, trying to make a decent living.

Later in the war, the Japanese became antagonistic. Those caught plotting against them were dealt with mercilessly.

Prior to the invasion, the Japanese had known the hamlet well. Japanese spies had entrenched themselves among the business community. Ample intelligence was at their fingertips, provided by their comrade working in plantations and estates before war broke out.

A large chunk of land such as the Kabota Estate, the Kuhara Rubber plantation and the coconut estate were under Japanese enterprise. As the war dragged on, the Japanese became belligerent and treated the populace badly. A cloud of fear began to develop amongst the local inhabitants.

Stephen Tan, a local Chinese staying in Tanjung Batu was duly appointed as the Kapitan Cina. He had a close rapport with the Japanese military until the kampitai suspected that he was a member of the Chinese Patriotic Society.

The Japanese suspected that the rich Chinese in the community had collected funds for the China cause. Several were investigated and detained. Those involved were: Mr. Woo Kon Hoi, Mr. Shim Thiam Su and several other local Chinese staying at Sin On. The detainees were then tortured and with the information given to them, more arrests were carried out. Seven men and a woman were brought up to a hill some seven miles from the junction of Apas and Tinagat road. They were forced to dig a large hole and summarily executed and dumped into the same hole. The Chinese at Tinagat named that area as 'Massacre Hill'.

The massacre hill at Kampong Tinagat Tawau Sabah

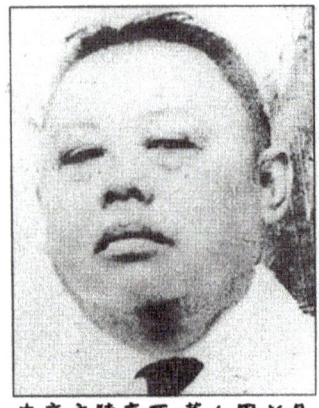

史帝文陳高西 華人甲必丹
Stephen Tan – Chinese Kapitan

Rev Father Bekama the Rector of Holy Trinity Church offered prayers at the site after the war, praying for the souls of the massacred victims. Courtesy of Mr Chia Siew Boon

News of the massacre spread like wildfire. The populace began to hoard whatever of value. Extra rice and food were also buried to prevent the Japanese from confiscating them. The dollar currency used during the British time was stopped from circulation. Japanese banana currency was used instead. Successful businessmen had their gold and dollars hidden in dug-up holes. This was done secretly at night. Some of the hidden valuables were not traceable after the owners' death.

During the occupation, the Japanese built a hospital just after the Tungku Osman Bridge. It was close to the present SMK Tawau vicinity and Kampong Java. Doctor Hisammoto was the Japanese doctor stationed at the Hospital.

In front of the hospital stood a fort where Japanese soldiers stood guard. The hospital was about five kilometers from the town.

The war continued unabated, the allied soldiers were on their final push to destroy the Japanese garrison and facilities. The bombing of the town began on the 18 April and ended in May.

As the bombers came, the warning siren broke the calm serene atmosphere of Tawau town and the people ran for cover. The liberator bomber suddenly emerged from the sky like a hawk and began dropping their deadly cargoes on the town. The Japanese defenses was no match for the flying fortress. The town was completely in flames, and not a soul was in sight. The siren stopped, and the populace began to come out to witness the destructive force of the bombing on their town.

The war ended in 1945 after two atomic bombs were dropped at Hiroshima and Nagasaki. The Japanese finally surrendered.

Lt. Colonel JA England, an Australian army officer from Sandakan was dispatched to Tawau. He was to supervise the Japanese final surrender in Tawau.

In the interim, many of the local spies and collaborators for the Japanese secretly disappeared.

These collaborators could be used as witnesses at the newly formed war tribunals.

Major Sugasaki Moriyuki with his 2900 soldiers and Japanese civilians were taken as prisoners. They were dispatched to Jesselton by ship to be repatriated back to Japan.

Japanese soldiers and their families being deported back to Japan

I could still remember the fortress near the hospital. Remnants of Japanese helmet and spent cartridges could still be found.

The Japanese legacy

The family of Stephen Tan in Tawau at the graveyard of Josephine's husband who died of illness.

EPISODE 6

Japanese final surrender in Tawau

Lt. Colonel JA England, an Australian army officer from Sandakan was dispatched to Tawau. He was to supervise the Japanese final surrender in Tawau.

In the interim, many of the local spies and collaborators for the Japanese secretly disappeared, knowing that the Allied would detain them to stand as witnesses at the newly formed war tribunals.

Major Sugasaki Moriyuki with his 2900 soldiers and Japanese civilians were taken as prisoners. They were dispatched to Jesselton by ship to be repatriated back to Japan.

John Gilbert Bridger

John Gilbert Bridger in military uniform. By courtesy of Eddy Sophian Pulle

John Gilbert Bridger as a young man was among the military personnel who came with the military contingent to South East Asia. He was dispatched to Singapore and British North Borneo in 1946. He was holding the rank of a warrant officer first class. From Singapore, the military attached him to the war crimes tribunal in Jesselton and Labuan.

John was born in Shanghai and stayed there as a young boy. John's father worked in Shanghai China for the American Express company. John father sent him to the United Kingdom for further study. After graduation from the school of higher learning, he wanted to travel around the world. After putting all his option on the table, he discovered that the military was the only institution that could fulfil his dream. He enlisted in the British Army, just as the war was about to end. After the war, John was searching for his father, but no clue of his whereabouts.

Railway car jeep used by John Gilbert Bridger travelling from Jesselton to Papar by rail before being transfered to Tawau in 1947.

The railway jeep used by John Gilbert Bridger, travelling from Jesselton to Papar from 1946 to 1947

In Jesselton 1946

J.G. Bridger, 1st Class Warrant Officer, attached with the War Crime Tribunals stationed in both Jesselton and Labuan Island in 1946 with two locals. By courtesy of Datuk Clement Jaikul

Prior to his decommission from the military in 1947, he was instructed to manage the Kabota Estate in Tawau. Following decommissions, John joined BAL estate as a young planter at Table, Mostyn and a second stint Table Abaca Estate.

Borneo Abaca Plantation Limited Tawau Sabah
(Jute division)

Borneo Abaca.

John was well liked by the local community. With his social standing, he was able to befriend many of the local associates and local well-known personals of Tawau.

In 1963, he decided to apply for citizenship and was approved. He was one of the very few expatriates who opted not to return to their original country. He married a local lady and had several children.

Mr. John Gilbert Bridger and his family taken in Tawau (Standing from left: Michael, Henny, Eddy, Jean, Mae and Richard: sitting from left Datin Jainab, Peter and Datuk Gilbert Bridger. courtesy of Eddy Sophian Pulle

After working for BAL estate for several years, he eventually opted for an early retirement and joined Sasco, a subsidiary of Hap Seng Company as their Plantation Consultant. Besides the said company, Datuk John Gilbert Bridger was also the board of Directors of several Government Link Companies such as KPD, the Tun Fuad and Tun Razak Cocoa Project, Sakilan Desa and others. He died in Tawau in the year 2000 and buried at the expatriate cemetery at BAL Estate.

Mr. Horace Traulson

Mr. and Mrs. Horace Traulson and Carol. By courtesy of Carl Traulson

Mr. Horace Traulson set his first footstep in Tawau in the year 1949. He came with his wife and three-year old cute little Carol born in Eustis Florida America. He was employed by an American company who had just bought a large track of the jute plantation from a Japanese company at BAL estate.

Mr. Traulson, an American, was assigned to foresee the newly acquired piece of property. The company thrived for several years until a sudden outbreak of a disease called Bonchitop struck the plantation. Reeling from the outbreak, the company could not sustain the loss. They had no choice but to reduce the monthly emolument of the workforce to half. Mr. Horace Traulson and the workers were not happy with the reduction in remuneration and he decided to leave the company for good.

The company was sold to BAL estate and the beginning of an extensive replanting scheme by the new management. They planted jute, rubber trees, cocoa and oil palm. Mr. Horace Traulson decided to stay put and take up residence at the Tawau rest house for a year.

He knew that Tawau as a young town had ample opportunities that had no limit except the skies. His premonition came true when he was offered to open an area at Brantian prefecture.

Mrs. Traulson, the dedicated housewife who stood by her husband through thick and thin.

Mr. Horace Traulson, associates and workers in Brantian camp. By courtesy of Carl Traulson

With stock and barrel, he brought his family and young Carol to the deepest jungle of North Borneo at Brantian hamlet. He began the new enterprise, called the Brantian Estate Timber Company in 1952. It was a difficult venture, as there was no proper road to enter the jungle proper. He had to use a boat going upstream through the Kalabakan River.

His American pioneering instinct helped him to take the risk which no locals dare to undertake. After finalizing all the teething problem, he finally succeeded in putting his foothold.

I could still recall one early morning when dad got an urgent call in 1957. Dad told me he had to rush to Brantian to deliver a baby of Mrs. Traulson. He had to go by boat as there was no road. It was only in the late sixties that gravel road was constructed.

Mr. Traulson reared domestic animals and built a small self-contained farm to sustain his family livelihood. He brought in cows and buffaloes; in addition to the plentiful of wild animals roaming in the jungle proper. He began to exploit the timber stand accorded to him, and brought in some heavy equipment.

Carl and his younger brother in Brantian Estate in Tawau. By courtesy of Carl Traulson

His first son Carl was born in Jesselton in 1950. Subsequently, his other sibling Tom and Richard were both born in Tawau in 1957 and 1964 respectively. The children were brought up in a jungle scene scenario and had adapted their way of life in the jungle of Borneo.

The jungle of Borneo

After toiling for eleven years, they were directed to abandon the area due to the Malaysian Indonesian confrontation that started in 1963. I came to know from workers of the camp that Mr. Traulson released his buffaloes in the jungle of Brantian and many became wild and roaming into the surrounding jungle.

Mr. Horace Traulsen is testing the soil texture in the field in Tawau. By courtesy of Carl Traulson

Mr. Traulson celebrating his birthday. On the left Datuk Jeffrey Yee Lung Fook and on the right is his friend Mr. John Gilbert Bridger. By courtesy of Carl Traulson

Mr. Horace then started another company called Karito Estate just above the hamlet of BAL. His new-found enterprise was quite close to Tawau town. It gave him a golden opportunity to mix with the locals, the expatriate and the planters at the Tawau Sports Club and the Tawau Yacht Club.

Carl, who used to live in the jungle had no choice but to adapt to his new surroundings. It gave him the opportunity to mix around with the youth of Tawau.

On his birthday, he was surprised to see a new bicycle beside the corner of his room. He thanked his dad and quickly jumped on his bicycle for a round spin around the house. Mr. Traulson knew that his son had grown up, and needed something to tame his adventurous spirit. The bicycle gave him an opening to explore every nook and corner of the town. Not satisfying his audacious spirit, he cycled right up to Semporna, a coastal town of more than one hundred and seven kilometers away. It was a gravel link road currently under construction. A Philippine construction company called CDCP was given the task to seal the road.

The Kalumpang Bridge was not built yet. A barge was used to ferry vehicles and workers of PWD. On both sides of the road were nothing else except tall trees that stood magnificently on both sides.

Moving On

There were very few vehicles except the company and PWD Lorries.

Wild boars in the jungle of Borneo

Wild boars were plentiful and could be seen in the jungle fringes. Carl did a feat which none of the locals ever dare to venture. He once said to my late sister Cabrini that was the last time he ever dared to undertake. After resting several months to recoup his painful sores, he continued to move around with his bicycles visiting friends and family members. I was with the Tawau Youth Club movement, and one of our youth programs was to organize a bicycle race competition in celebration of the Queen's birthday. I was surprised to register an American boy who wanted to take part in the race. At first, I didn't know who he was until I saw the name Traulson. It suddenly came to my mind of a gentleman whom I knew when I was a boarder at Holy Trinity School Tawau. During that time, we had a big job, given by the priest to clear up the Holy Trinity Secondary School compound that was planted with coconuts.

It was a mammoth task to clear the area. Each coconut tree had to be uprooted. It took us days to uproot one coconut tree. Our work was made easy when Mr. H. Traulsen came to save the day. He provided us with a monkey jack where we could pull the trees and dislodge the entire roots.

I knew that this young man must be the son of Mr. Horace Traulsen. Anyway, he did not come first, but came in seven, and got a consolation prize. Encik Tahir from the PWD won the first price.

Carl Traulsen and his family in the USA. By courtesy of Carl Traulson

Carl on his electric bicycle. Not in Tawau but in America

    Carol, an elder sister of Carl, also had an adventurous spirit and used to farm life. She was a typical American farm girl who enjoyed the outdoor life, amongst the wild jungle of Borneo. Trained by her father, she had no fear of making use of the farm equipment such as the tractor and JCB.

    Mr. Horace Traulsen was well like and very active in his social life amongst the local. Because of his generous character, he provided his expertise in the landscaping of schools and recreational areas of Tawau. Part of the beautification of the coastal seafront was a result of his hard work. The Tawau Municipal Council named the area as "Taman Traulsen" When Mr. Traulson died of old age, the family sold their properties and moved back to the state and left Sabah for good.

Taman Traulson in Tawau 2013

EPISODE 7

Tawau after the Second World War

Reeling from the destruction of Tawau, the Chinese community began to rebuild their shop houses at the seafront. They were trying to start their shattered, life caused by the Japanese occupation. The allied forces occupying the town had to construct the administrative centre. The British Military Administrative took over the lease from the custodians of enemy property. Along the Dunlop Street stood several wooden shop houses.

Old shop houses at Jalan Chester Tawau Sabah

Moving On

Then in the wee hours of 1953, another disaster struck the town. It was not from bombing, but a spark of fire that engulfed most of the shop houses at the seafront.

None was spared except an old Chinese temple. The authorities had no choice but to build two rows of shop houses along Jalan Kuhara. A location closed to our school at Holy Trinity, Tawau. The Chinese shopkeepers continued their business uninterrupted. Most of the import finished products were from China.

Temporary shops built along Jalan Kuhara in 1953

The Chinese community gradually began to exhilarate their business enterprise. Many of them were involved in barter trade with Indonesia and the Philippines. They exported local products such as birds' nest and other jungle products to China. Many were successful as they expand their business in commodities, hardware and other essential goods. The Koh Bak Chin family took up the fishing business as their core income.

The town food stalls by the sea side

I watched the town growing. The town has changed since my last visit in 2018. I could not recognize many of the iconic places I used to know. Driving around town is another challenge. The roads have changed. Not the one I used to know in the seventies.

The people of this town are blessed with an abundance of natural resources. Timber was once the economic factor, followed by cocoa. Now oil palm plays an important part in the economy of Tawau. Due to the economic sustainability, the price of land and other properties have shot up.

Foreign investment keeps pouring in, and many young men and women are able to find proper jobs.

The expatriates from the timber industry such as Bombay Burma Trading Cooperation, the plantation sector and local government dignitaries frequently met at the Tawau Sports Club, The Tawau Yacht Club and the Tawau Golf Club. These were the only recreational spots that act as a melting pot for their weekends' escapee. On Saturdays and weekend holidays, local band accompanied by talented singers filled the air of merrymaking throughout the night.

Mr. Harry Ferdinand

One Musical band that stood above the rest, was a musical band led by Mr. Harry Ferdinand and his talented children. They could sing beautifully to entertain the members.

Mr. Ferdinand was born in Singapore. His mother was an Afghan mix with Terengganu Malay. His father a Dutch Burgher was from Ceylon. Mr. Ferdinand came to North Borneo in 1947 and later went to Singapore in 1949 to marry his wife miss Carman, a mixture of Dusun and Pilipino, born in Kudat. Mr. Ferdinand was attached to the Public Works department. During his free time, he helped to train and referee the boxing enthuses in Tawau. He was assisted by Teddy Usbah.

Madam Carman Lucy Santos and her children

The picture was taken in Lahad Datu (1956) with Rev Father Bekama, Mr. and Mrs. Harry Ferdinand, Mr. and Mrs. Braganza and other family friends

As the town expanded, many of the old semi wooden buildings were gone. The rich agricultural soil provided plantation to extend their acreage.

The fishing ground of the country was virtually untapped, and the Teo Chew's clan was good at it. Besides other business such as hardware, sundry goods, the opening of timber areas and large plantation created a financial business boom.

Being a Tawau native boy since young, I came to know many of the successful and well-known businessmen. Such as Lau Jit Poh, Teck Guan, Sim Mong Piak, Sim Hua Seng, Mark Pang and Sons, Lim Man Kui, Sim Chin Piang, Yong Luk, Man Tung Sing, William Thien, Liew Kim Do, Ales Pang, Edwin Chan, Joseph Lee, Anthony Chan, Philip Pang, Teo Han Ching and many others who had contributed the economic pulse of Tawau Town.

Apart from the Chinese enterprise, known natives were: Tawakal trading, Azura, Awadan and sons Datuk Abu Bakar Tintingan, Datuk Kassim Kamidin, Datuk Panglima Ahmad Ayid and Ahmad Daeng Mapata.

In the eighties and nineties, other enterprises from Sarawak and West Malaysia began to spread their wings to Tawau. From a small village, the town has grown into a municipality.

Businessmen such as Tan Sri Lau Gek Poh, Datuk Sri Panglima Hong Teck Guan, Hiew Fook Reality and many Chinese traders involved were able to expand their business into a large conglomerate. The landscape of Tawau Town completely changed. Empty plots of land belonging to Karim Pah, Kubota, Kuhara Apes, North Road are making way for development.

The area was known as Karim Pah.

I could still recall those early days when Mr. Hong Teck Guan was just a small business sundry goods dealer. Besides Tawau, he was operating a small shop at the timber village of Wallace Bay in 1954. Now his company has grown into a big conglomerate that deals with timber, plantation, Cocoa manufacturing, sundry shops and housing development.

TAN SRI LAU GEK POH

I salute Tan Sri Lau Gek Poh for his effort to put Tawau as one of the most progressive towns in Sabah. He reinvested and built one of the biggest housing estates in Tawau. Besides Tawau, the Hap Seng Consolidated Berhad encompasses several companies such as Hap Seng Plantation, Automotive, Building Materials and Fertilizer Trading.

Hap Seng started with a humble beginning. It has now grown into one of the biggest conglomerates in Malaysia and business ties in several other countries. It started with its timber operation in the early days in the Tawau Residency. With its highly motivated workforce and expertise in the timber operation, it was awarded a large chunk of areas for the extraction of timbers by several government bodies and individuals.

Tan Sri Lau Gek Poh JP, PGDK, SPDK and SMN

I could still recall the days when I met Mr. Lau Gek Poh in his small wooden office near to Sim Mong Piak warehouse. I went to see him to hand over a quotation of wire rope which he had requested from Service and Trading. A company started by Mr. John Anselmi and my father Peter Raymond Lai in 1963

Mr. Lau Gek Poh knew that the timber areas in the state could not sustain indefinitely. As a result of his vision, he reinvested into the construction industry, plantation, fertilizers and building materials. His intuition came right on track as the timber boom began to decrease in production and Tawau became an agricultural town.

Hap Seng company has provided job opportunity to many locals, and one of the biggest job providers in the construction section, the plantation and its mammoth head office in Kota Kinabalu and in Petaling Jaya Jalan P. Ramli.

A soft-spoken man, I had the opportunity meeting him the second time with my St Patrick building fund Chairlady Puan Christina Liew. Without hesitation, he gave us fifty thousand ringgits on the spot and reiterated that our team of fundraiser should be commended for doing all the hard work.

Tan Sri Lau Gek Poh knew the importance of education. A country cannot prosper without an educated workforce. With this philosophic thought, he had all his life provided funds to schools, churches, temples and other worthwhile institution. SRJK Sin Hwa Chinese Primary School in Tawau has been provided financial help for many years. As a token of appreciation, the school board has erected a bronze stature right in front of the school building.

The immortalized statue of Tan Sri Lau Gek Poh situated at Sin Hwa Chinese Primary School Tawau

Recently I had the opportunity to glance at the life of Tan Sri at the Gek Poh building in Tawau. A big building that commands a beautiful view of the Cowie Harbor. The first floor of the building is an open space for community use. The first and second room of the second floor are used to keep historical documents and memento, nicely kept in glass shelves.

Entrance to Tan Sri Lau Gek Poh foundation building in Tawau Sabah

Tan Sri Lau Gek Poh personal calligraphy at Gek Poh Building in Tawau

Tan Sri Lau Gek Poh personal collection.

The megalith erected at the compound of the late
Tan Sri Lau Gek Poh foundation in Tawau

Tan Sri Lau Gek Poh was assisted by his nephew Tan Sri Lau Chu Khun who has been with him throughout the rapid expansion of the company and the driving force that made the company as it is today.

Menara Hap Seng, Jalan P. Ramlee Kuala Lumpur

The Plaza Shell, the Hap Seng building in Kota Kinabalu. 2018

Moving On

The Hap Seng Group of companies

DATUK SRI PANGLIMA HONG TECK GUAN

Datuk Sri Panglima Hong Teck Guan

Datuk Sri Hong Teck Guan was a simple and modest man. In 1926, he went to Kedah to study and worked there for a while. Then later in the years, he went to Kuching Sarawak to meet his uncle to learn about fishing. Several years later, he was able to own several fishing boats for the fishing business.

He travelled far and wide, up to the Borneo coast in Sandakan. Whilst in Sandakan, world war two broke out and he could not return to Kuching with his fishing boats. Stranded, he had a force to look east and landed in Tawau.

With his fishing fleet in Tawau, he continued to pursue his dream and became a very successful fishing pioneer in the industry. He had a very big ice factory at the far end of Kampung Tintingan, formerly known as Ice Box by the local people. I could still remember Teck Guan aerated water in bottles which they used to sell in those early days. Besides the above, he was the agent for Holden cars, Chocolate industry and several commodities. As his business expanded, he reinvested into the plantation, hardware, timber operation and housing development.

The family was well known in Tawau and his wife used to accompany my mom Gabriella to seek donation for schools and churches. Datuk Sri Panglima Hong Teck Guan was one of the founders of SRK Yuk Chin School and a co-founder of the Sabah Chinese High School with Datuk Hiew Fook. He was also the generous contributor to a school named Kelombong Che Hwa Primary School in Kota Kinabalu. As a result of his generous philanthropist, the State Government awarded him his daturship. Before he died in 1997, he was converted to Christianity by Rev Father Tung and buried at the Christian Cemetery in Tawau.

Che Hwa Chinese Primary School in Kolombong that the Late Datuk Sri Panglima Hong Teck Guan contributed

Datuk Hiew Fook

Hiew Fook

Datuk Hiew Fook

Followed by the two well-known Chinese businessmen was Datuk Hiew Fook. Datuk Hiew Fook was the man behind the establishment and creation of a full-fledged Chinese secondary school in Tawau. It was named the Sabah Chinese High School Tawau.

I met his son Hiew Ming Yong to seek donation for the St Patrick Primary School. He was generous and gave us a lot of support. The first Hotel of international standard was built by Mr. Hiew Ming Yong called Marco Polo.

Hiew Fook Memorial Hall standing firm and strong at the Sabah Chinese High School Tawau Sabah

The Sabah Chinese High School in Tawau

Tawau as it looks in 2013. A booming town that has a large potential for development and investment

I was still in deep thought, reminiscing past memories when the call for boarding woke me up. I thought I was still riding on an old bus in Tawau which I used to ride in the fifties. Instead, I was walking towards a Boeing plane ready to fly direct to Kota Kinabalu from Tawau.

Tawau Transport that belongs to Mr Yong

The only bus company I knew when I was in school.

EPISODE 8

Arriving in the national's capital

We landed at Kota Kinabalu international airport. Our children were there to meet us. On the way home to Luyang Perdana, I noticed many of the known landmarks had changed. The old iconic building I used to know had gone. Beautiful architectural skyscraper dotted the skyline. The kampong air houses in the water had left just a few.

For several days, we tried to get use to our new environment. After a week we began to explore the area and trying to get to know our immediate neighbor. We dared not walk too far, as we might lose our way in this strange surrounding.

After a month of stay in Kota Kinabalu, I began to miss my hometown in Tawau at Taman Bestari. I missed all the usual thing I used to do. Such as spending time in the kebun or at the Tanjung Hot spring golf club. My favorite of all was to walk casually under the tall trees. Back to nature, where I could relax and watch the birds flying up in the sky. I was never bored as all the facilities for a retiree is within the palm of my hand.

Here in Kota Kinabalu, was a completely different game, a different scenario to let the day passed by.

What I need now, is to bring myself to a new consciousness. To begin a fresh start to make myself a part of Kota Kinabalu.

Restless at home, we tried to explore beyond our Taman. We went direct to the Penampang road and took a long walk to Lido. We wanted to see the well-known market, in the hope of seeing familiar faces.

We kept on going, but the distance was too much for us. Being tired and thirsty, we reverted back to our home. In the morning I went to the jogging track in front of the Agriculture office. Many early morning joggers were already there with their cars parking randomly with no concern of the "No Parking" sign. I was taken aback when I saw cars parking on the roundabout and double parking as well. Probably, it's the Sabahan way of life.

Searching for a house.

For several weeks I browsed through the internet to find houses for sale. There were many, but either the price was too expensive or the location did not fit for our taste.

Our search brought us to many housing estates new and old. We went right to Inanam town and went to Jalan Kiasom to search for a well-known housing estate. We found one and the price offered was within our reach. But after consulting with Nicholas my son in law, the idea was put off. First, it was quite a distance, and to travel on that long road might be too stressful for us. Night time travel was another factor, especially when the road was narrow and no street lights. Thirdly, the traffic jam during working hours was a nightmare.

We went to inspect another house close at Likas shown to me by my sister Gloria. It was a detached house but the surrounding environment was not conducive to our liking. Besides that, the whole house was affected by a colony of termites.

It was only after the third month that we finally found a suitable terrace corner house at Taman BDC Kolombong. It is a small terrace house, but it's good enough for both of us.

Looking back on the earlier era of Jesselton

The younger generation of today has attained much of the development pioneered by the last generation.

Moving On

In this twenty-first century, the technology is so advanced that people of yesteryear had never dreamed off.

The older generation like my grandfather Austin Lai Man might have a tough time in 1926. He was on his prime life, struggling to make a decent living, by working for the Charted Company in Jesselton transporting commodities from far-flung areas to the port.

Basic infrastructure was nominal. Facilities like electricity and water were non-existence. Many nearby towns and villages had to use kerosene lamps. There was no sealed road except narrow footpath and gravel road mainly used by buffaloes and horses.

Api Api in the bygone era in 1930. Courtesy of Madam Evelyn Lim

The old railway line of the Charted Company. The background depicts the Gaya Island

By courtesy of Madam Evelyn Lim

Api Api in the bygone era before the war, by courtesy of Madam Evelyn Lim

Jesselton after the war, by courtesy of Madam Evelyn Lim

The only long-distance cheap transport available was the North Borneo railway line which started from Tanjung Aru and ended at Tenom.

Likewise, they were no dispensary to provide proper medical care to the populace. They had to travel far and wide on foot to seek medical help.

To provide better health to the people of far-flung villages. The health department introduced the flying doctor service in the seventies.

The flying doctor service in Sabah

With the flying doctor weekly service introduced, the kampong folks were relieved of the need to travel far and wide to get their medical supplies. My buddy Joseph Jominol was attached to the flying doctor team for a year. He visited many of the far-flung areas such as in Kinabatangan hamlet and islands.

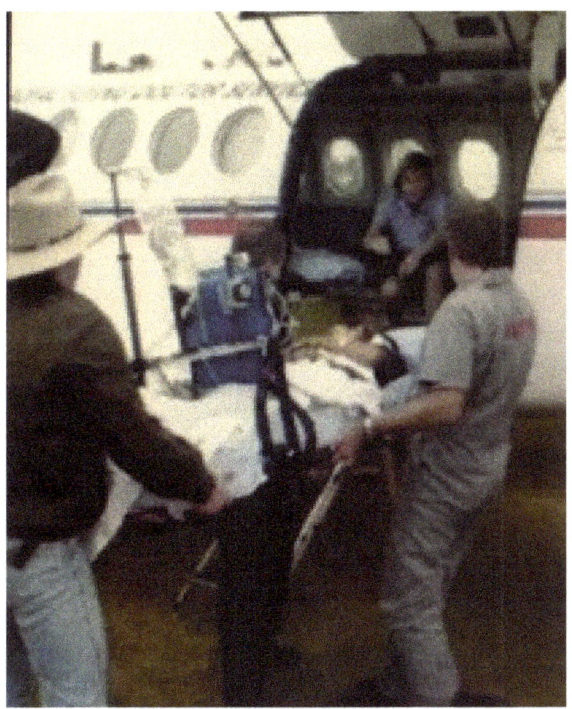

The sick being ferried for further treatment

Joseph could still rekindle some experiences whilst flying up in the sky with the medical team. Occasionally, fear came to his mind when up from with the unpredictable nasty weather. There were times when the weather changed dramatically. A moment of panic to the passengers, as the helicopter tried to maneuver from danger.

Throughout the years, the flying doctor service had reduced its normal flights. This was due to the accessibility of newly constructed roads.

The final straw was in the year 2015 when it ceased completely. According to the medical department, many of the far-flung kampongs have now reachable by road. Medical units on the four-wheel drive vehicle have now being assigned to Kampongs. They could extend their visit longer periods to serve the kampong folks better. In spite of the danger, Joseph had enjoyed his weekly flying visit. Those ordeals that he had gone through gave him once in a lifetime experience.

He was relieved when his service at the flying doctor team ended and put his feet back on solid ground.

Api Api town/Jesselton

The capital of Sabah was once called API API, then Jesselton and finally Kota Kinabalu. How it came about, was through the spoken language of the natives that depicted a certain area of location. It was then conveniently used to name it, such as the name of a river called Sungai API API or the seaside tree called API API or Deasoka which means below the coconut trees in the Bajau Language.

Another name was Singga Mata or transit eye literally means pleasing to the eye given by fisherman from Gaya Island.

Gaya Island was first located and used as the administrative centre by the British North Borneo Company in 1897. The settlement was short live. A local Bajau Suluk inhabitant called Mat Salleh did not see eye to eye with the British administrator.

As a result of his misunderstanding with the British, Mat Salleh and his men revolted. They torched the whole settlement and escaped. The populace opposite the island (now Jesselton) saw the big flame and shouted API API. Hence Jesselton was once called Api Api.

Mat Salleh and his gang escaped to Tambunan with his men. The British and some policemen were directed to search for him. He was finally found in the Tambunan hamlet. A short encounter occurred, and Mat Salleh and several of his men were killed.

Mat Saleh memorial in Tambunan

The revolt against the British on Gaya Island caused great uneasiness to the British personnel. The management finally decided to move out and relocated the settlement at Gantian Bay now Sepanger Bay. The company found that the area was not suitable, and directed Sir Henry Walter to locate a suitable site. After months of search, he identified a small fishing village called API API now Jesselton.

In 1899 several shops were built by some Chinese traders. Most of the goods were imported from China and Hong Kong.

After the war the locals met the Australian soldiers. How pathetic these people were? Courtesy of Datuk Wilfred Lingham

The war that ended in 1945 had caused great destruction to the settlement and the Charted Company had no means to rebuild the wartorn country. The new settlement was named Jesselton after Sir Charles Jessel gave it to the British Crown in 1946.

Australian military in North Borneo. Courtesy of Madam Evelin Lim

Moving On

Australian soldiers first taste of local brew.
Courtesy of Madam Evelyn Lim

In 1967 Jesselton was renamed as Kota Kinabalu which derived the name from the name "Aki Nabalu" meaning the revered place for the death. Aki means ancestors or grandfather. Nabalu is the name of the mountain in the Dusun language.

Kota Kinabalu which had gone through thick and thin, has made a phenomenal improvement and recovers from the destruction of war. Road infrastructure from Kota Kinabalu to the rest of towns in Sabah has made inroad and is feasible to travel to all the other towns in the state of Sabah by road.

A month after my stay in Kota Kinabalu, I decided to make a visit to an area called Tanjung Aru Beach. I needed to reinstate my footprint in that area. That was where I met my love and long-lasting partner. It was also the place where many young lovers of Kota Kinabalu met and set hours looking at the silhouette sundown. In silent, they gazed at Gaya Island on their sight, not knowing the emancipation that the island had gone through in the past century.

The Tanjung Aru Beach in Jesselton North Borneo.
By courtesy of Madam Evelyn Lim

Next to the beach was the cultural village known as the Prince Philip Park. A site to commemorate the visit of Prince Philip of the United Kingdom to Sabah. A fun area for families and visitors alike to witness and enjoy the iconic model of indigenous tribe building to portray the people's way of life. A place where most of the people could spend their holiday and free time with their families and meet friends.

Sadly, throughout the years the area was left abandoned and in a dire disrepair. The authorities have no intention of reviving the once beautiful spot or to cherish the legacy of Prince Philip. Instead, a new project is in the pipeline to transform the whole area with high end living and international class hotel and recreation purposes for the people of Sabah.

The wooden walkway at the park.

The proposed new park at Tanjung Aru

Besides the once famous Tanjung Aru beach, there is another recreational site along the Likes Bay highway.

Ordinary shops mostly run by families are gradually being absolute and added to the history of the past. Instead of big malls and international class hotels of five stars dotted the skyline.

The once water village called Kampung air where most of the Chinese and their indigenous natives lived near to the shore had gone.

Kampung Air or water village of the past in Jesselton North Borneo. By courtesy of Madam Evelyn Lim

The actual shoreline was just a stone throw from the Sacred Heart Cathedral. In the early eighties, the government had decided to reclaim the whole area. Notices were given to house owners to vacate their houses along the kampong air community.

In the year 2001, most of the houses at the seafront had gone except a few. Kota Kinabalu has begun its modernization. It has not stopped but continues to expand. Within a couple more years, there will be more flyover within the city areas to ease up the traffic congestion.

The city of Kota Kinabalu in 2017

Kota Kinabalu is now a city and it is the administrative city of the government, hence the Capital of Sabah.

Many facilities are upgraded to encourage foreign visitors to visit Sabah "The Land below the Wind". Foreign tourists who visit here will spur the economic activity of the state.

The nearest hamlet of Kota Kinabalu is the Penampang area. An area one time was called the breadbasket of the state. Padi fields were found everywhere, as far as the eye could see. Now the area is being developed, and many housing estates pop up at every nook and corner of Penampang. A phenomenon that has happened in every part of the world as the population increases.

EPISODE 9

The earliest settlers in Borneo

As a little kid growing up in this wonderful world, I often marvel at what it was like beyond the solar system. I wondered as I was watching millions of twinkling lights up in the sky. I was baffled and bewildered at the millions of bright illuminations hovering up above. I had no answer, but to look in awe. I was naive and innocent. Waiting to pass the time, as the world continues to move on.

It's my curiosity that encouraged me to seek the hidden tales beyond my comprehension. Stories long are forgotten, but still important to provide food for thoughts to the new generation. Some sprinkling of historical facts would be appropriated to summaries and made known.

This work is long and tedious, but I will remain committed until it's completed. Being a retiree gave me the time and prospects to travel to every nook and corner of this beautiful Sabah. I have visited most of it for the last four years and had accrued untold stories.

I could not have made it on my personal effort, if not for the right channel, called the Sabah Government Pensioner Association. It's through this association that makes my work easier and a gratitude that I hold dear to express my sincere thanks to all those concerned

Moving On

The indigenous people.

In the earlier part of human civilization, the world landmass was a free for all to explore, venture, conquer and settle.

This tiny unknown land called North Borneo was not exempted from the cradle of human civilization. It has moved on to the tune of human drama for thousands of years.

The origin of the earlier settlers might have migrated from the same source: the Asian region.

Borneo had been their home from time long-established.

Where did the people of Borneo come from? What made them migrate and left their country of origin? Taking the risk of facing the unknown and uncharted territory, a question which has been on the public mind.

The tribe in Borneo. Courtesy of Madam Evelyn Lim

Several types of research were made by world prominence anthropologist. They found that these people might have migrated from the continent of Asia thousands of years ago. The demography of human population that existed millions of years ago, in every corner of the world gave us the clue of the migration odyssey.

There were no written records to verify these migrations of human species. Only traces and analyses of artifacts found in various parts of Borneo in resemblance, found in other parts of the world. We might also wonder why these people left their country of origin. What was it that spurred them to travel under such circumstances? Was it environmental or human catastrophe such as illnesses, war or ravaged by a volcanic eruption?

To keep the story local, let us explore the people of North Borneo.

They were many tribes that coexisted for many generations. The main tribes of North Borneo were the Kadazan, Dusun, Orang Sungai, Muruts and other indigenous that came mainly from the neighboring vast land of South East Asia.

To interpret the cultural heritage of these tribes, we could verify their similarity from their custom, dress and behaviors.

For thousands of years, these people were living in a cluster of villages. They sustained their livelihood by making full use of the land and the natural habitats of the locality, reaping natural products such as fish and wild animals.

Barter trading was the norm of the day called Tamu Ground. Their beliefs were centered on the natural phenomena of the earth. Praying for good weather and for the abundance of their crops which we now called the Harvest Festival. Such cultural events encompassed in many parts of the world.

The houses they built reflect on the environment they lived. Locally available materials were mainly used, found close to the settlement. They lived in the cluster of villages and in longhouses for self-protection from other warlike tribes. To sustain their group, large families were the norm. The greater in numbers, the greater the chance of the tribe's survival.

The Neolithic periods of North Borneo

Had the tribes of the Austronesian migrant of Sahul, during the Neolithic period travelled up the stream of the Labuk and Kinabatangan River? After their long journey, they decided to rest on the river bank. Probably there were several boats that travelled on different parts of Borneo.

An indigenous tribe from Borneo. Courtesy of Evelyn Lim

The Kinabatangan and Labuk River were once the source of human settlement. They were called as Orang Sungai, Muruts, Bisaya and other ethnic tribes.

The early tribe of North Borneo. Courtesy of Datuk Wilfred Lingham

Population increased, and sustainable resources decreased, they moved to areas such as Keningau, Ranau, Tenom and other parts of North Borneo. Small hamlet began to develop and self-contained for all the needs to sustain the tribe. With their survival skills and knowledge accumulated over the years, they survived through agricultural produce and domestication of animals.

The warrior from Fujian

In the year 1408, a warrior from Fujian became the Raja of Kinabatangan. He was dispatched by the Ming Dynasty emperor. His mission was to find the precious treasure on top of Mount Kinabalu. They established the Mumiang settlement on the Kinabatangan River.

The warrior's sister married Ahmad who became the Sultan of Brunei. The warrior married Princes Ratna Dewi, the daughter of the first sultan of Brunei, Sultan Mohd Shah (1368-1402). After the demise of the warrior, Awang or Hiawang the son of the warrior was appointed as the Raja of Kinabatangan. The Labuk River became the main exploration site, for the assault to ascent Mount Kinabalu. Several expeditions were sent but failed to return. Soldiers and their potters whom were brought in from the ethnic tribe of Formosa (Taiwan) decided not to return to China due to Hiawang conversion to the Muslim religion.

Many of the soldiers and potters married local native women who were descendants of the Austronesian migrants of Sahul during the Neolithic period giving rise to the Kadazan/Dusun race.

Notably the ethnic Bundu of Kuala Penyu. There were many different ethnic tribes under the Kadazan/Dusun. Each as given by their neighbors on a subsequent location of their homes at Nunuk Ragang such as The Bundu, Ida'an, Bagak, Subpan, Liwan, Tuhawon, Rungus, Lobu, Mangka'ak, Rumanau, Kwijau. Tangaa Tolinting, Tagahas, Tambanuo and Bonggi. There was no written record but from words of mouth, attire, song or dance from old folks that still exist today. Traces of artifacts could still be found in the Kinabatangan and several locations in Sabah such as Madai cave at Kunak, Lahad Datu, Penampang area, Semporna and Tawau that depict of human existence thousands of years ago. Meanwhile, the areas as mentioned had not been fully explored and researched to substantiate the historical origin of the people of Borneo.

Foreign influence.

The Chartered Company played a major role to make their presence felt in North Borneo. After the Second World War, the British Crown took over North Borneo and became a colony. There was no political inclination amongst the races. The missionaries of the various denomination that came to the land, had played an important role in the social development of the indigenous people of Borneo. Their know-how and experience in promoting education, agricultural and economic matters had propelled the indigenous the knowledge and technical expertise to improve their livelihood.

It had also opened up a window of opportunities for the natives to excel themselves in the educational fields. Their livelihood began to improve as the basic education was introduced by the missionaries. The old traditional ways of living in kampongs or villages as they did in the past began to decline. Only in unreachable areas in far-flung villages, the old system continued to flourish.

The people became politically motivated when North Borneo joined the federation and formed Malaysia. The awakening in the political area began the introductory of ethnic groups in each area of interest. Each was trying to formulate their own cultural heritage. Hence racial political parties began to increase in this little state.

The British as the colonial power had given fewer emphasis on the development of the country. The state infrastructure during that era was limited.

Each town depended entirely on sea route. It took weeks or month to reach from one destination to the other. It was only at a later date, that railway was used as the cheapest form of transport. Other means of transport such as Dakota airways and steamship were introduced to ferry goods along the coastal towns of North Borneo, came at a later date. However, in the seventies, road infrastructure was improved thus providing another mode of transport to fill the needs of North Borneo at that time.

Nevertheless, the legacy the British had left us, was the civil service management.

Tan Sri Simon Sipaun, the former state secretary of Sabah could still rekindle the work culture of the British administration. A legacy that the state continues to emulate up to this very day.

During the colonial days, the education department was under the jurisdiction of the country and under British management. English was used as the mode of teaching in all schools. It was only in the year 1983 that transformation began to use Bahasa Malaysia as a medium of teaching and learning in all primary schools with the exception in Chinese schools.

Several private institutions run by missionaries and Chinese school were working hand in hand complimenting the government efforts to reduce illiteracy rate in the country. Vernacular Malay schools were undertaken by the government to facilitate other option for the Malay community. Kent College teachers training centre was the epic ground for Malay and Chinese education in the country. The Teachers training Gaya College continued with English as the lingual for those trained in the English language.

Many young Sabahan with the right qualification were sent to further their education overseas. They were expected to return with the right know-how to provide the necessary manpower to administer this emerging country.

However, despite the effort, it was not able to churn out enough to oversee the state's requirement. As an interim, the British had to bring in expertise from countries such as Ceylon, India, Hong Kong and the United Kingdom to fill in various government post. When Malaysia was formed, many came from West Malaysia to fill in the government top post. Much to the consternation of the local people. In the seventies and eighties, infrastructure began to develop and many remote areas were opened up for growth.

More development had been extended on reclaimed land as more business enterprise emerged.

The onslaught of world wars and the aftermath that followed during the last centuries, gave rise to nations forming the world body called the United Nation. Britain or the British Empire and many other European Countries had the large chunk of land mass that was colonized by them. Many countries, ranging from South East Asia to the African continent, were once under the domination of western civilization. These countries were given the choice and freedom to rule for themselves.

Newly minted leaders became to rule the day. Ravenousness, mismanagement and the like, caused problems reeling from natural resources being missused.

EPISODE 10

A window of North Borneo

In the past epoch, this little land mass called North Borneo was largely left to its idealist uninhabited piece of property. It was once supposedly ruled by the Sultan of Sulu or Brunei. Later a lease was given out to several European powers as stated in history. The British Chartered Company came to explore the viability of making use of its fertile land for its commercial purposes. The British Chartered Company ruled the State till 1942 when the country was subsequently occupied by the Japanese military on 16 December 1941.

After the Second World War in 1945, the company could not sustain its operation due to the high cost. It was then handed over to the British Crown and became the colony of the British Empire. Once again North Borneo was peaceful, and the populace lived in harmony accepting the British know how to administer the country.

In 1963, the population of North Borneo was slightly over a million. Its institution had not fully attained maturity for self-reliance. There was no university or institution of higher learning. Local leaders were not fully trained or experienced enough to lead the country. The British was conscious of its shortcoming and knew the capability of its people. Such basic prerequisite was not addressed. In spite of this concern and shortfall, they pressed on, without making further assessment of its future impact on the population.

To clear themselves of any future wrongdoing, they directed the United Nation to establish the Cobbold Commission. Knowingly or unknowingly, the people participated in the survey. It took them several weeks of fact-finding assignment to conclude. They declared to the general assembly of the united nation that the population of Sabah had accepted the merger.

The result of this declaration, Malaysia was formed on 16 September 1963.

Formation of Malaysia in 1963. Courtesy of Datuk Wilfred Lingham

The Malaysia agreement was then sealed. In addition to the agreement, certain special rights were given to both Sabah and Sarawak. Brunei refused to partake in the new union because the British had the high stake on this country. Singapore left after months of unreconciled bittering.

As Malaysia was on the threshold of being formed, our nearest neighbor Indonesia was agitated by the formation.

A brief war of words erupted and some skirmishes happened along its border towns, but it was more of a show of discontentment than of war. The brief clashes ended in the year 1966.

Furthermore, the Philippines unresolved claim to the state has not completely put to rest. It's an ongoing issue with no sign of light at the end of the tunnel. The faith of the country is moving in a direction of uncertainty. Only time will tell what the future would be for our beloved state.

At the onset of the formation, the populace of North Borneo had high hopes that better days were on the horizon.

Moving On

The first Sabah cabinet was formed in 1963 to cater for the needs of the populace.

The first cabinet in the state of Sabah. By courtesy of Mr. Andrew Lai

After decades of administration, the country had moved on uncharted territories. Leaders voted by the people began to put their self-interest first. The rich natural resources of the state went to the power behind the crown.

The agreement on the formation of the nation took a different course and deviated from its first charter. Cracks amongst the populace began to manifest, and the general public began to question the course of its destiny.

Several decades later, the people had to shoulder the burden and paid the political price of ambiguity.

Political issues and trail of indecisive policies from the top power began to emerge. Ideologies began to creep into the machinery of government and the ugly head of exploitation and chauvinism began to rule the day.

In the fourteenth general election on May the 9, 2018, the government of the day since 1963 lost its grip on power. A new government was born. It was a thought-provoking time to remedy the wrongdoings that the new government had in store.

From Perlis to Sabah a new breath of fresh air came thrashing in. The bad aura that had chocked the people was free. It was an unexpected event of a historical proposition that completely changed the scene of the nation. The people had spoken not through a revolution of arms uprising, but through the ballot box that every individual had played a role. To all our new generation, please remember this: The 9 of May 2018 was a historical event that stunts the world when a 92-year-old man, a former prime minister succeeded to serve the nation again. On the 16 of September 2018, the Prime Minister of Malaysia declared that both Sabah and Sarawak will be given their rights in accordance with the M63.

Mount Kinabalu in Kundasang Ranau Kota Kinabalu
to bring hope to the people of Sabah

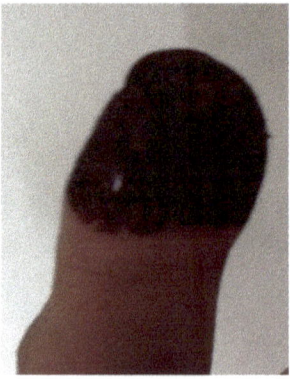

The mark that changed the moral landscape of Malaysia

EPISODE 11

Monsopiad Village in Penampang Hamlet

The village of Monsopiad in Penampang hamlet

The village of Monsopiad has situated at Penampang proper. It provides a clear picture and a clear understanding of the tribe that has lived in that area.

Indigenous tribe in North Borneo, courtesy of Datuk Wilfred Lingham

The site is situated in a small kampong called Kuai. The indigenous tribe was head-hunters. Tribal warfare between villages was the norm and the way of life. Sworn enemies caught would find their heads staked on poles, to be smoked and hung by the beam under the roof.

The house of Skull

Skulls of enemies hung by the beam under the roof

Testing of the home-made wine called Tapai

Village life was routine. Day in and day out, the tribes were on their normal round of simple daily chores.

On the way to the padi field. Courtesy of Datuk Wilfred Lingham

Women were kept busy out in the padi field, cooking meals and other chores for their families. Men were out hunting and keeping watch on the village perimeter to ensure no strangers or intruders impairing the safety of the tribe.

In the tribal village of Penampang. Courtesy of Datuk Wilfred Lingham

Children, as usual, would be indulged in their normal children past time. None could foresee that such a peaceful scene could suddenly be transformed into a tragic commotion.

Horror and calamity beyond their expectation suddenly broke the peaceful village. People were seen falling and died on the spot for no apparent reason. A hidden spiritual enemy was on the loose and prowled everywhere like the shadow of death.

Their spears, blowpipe and arrows were no match, as they could not see it. The situation was so deadly that the living burying the dead themselves were victims and died the next day. The village was temporarily abandoned by the survivors and built temporary village away from the epic centre of the tragedy.

House of Indigenous tribe in the bygone era in Penampang hamlet

None dare to venture in the kampong. They waited several months before entering the disaster zone. Several warriors were sent to examine the site. They finally returned to their villages after finding it was safe. Fearing for the recurrence of the past of the dreadful episode, the village decided to get the spiritual advice and expertise of the Bobohizans.

The priestess or Bobohizans

Bobohizans are high priest and well-respected village doctors. They played an integral part in the Kadazan Dusun society. They carried out rituals and acted as intermediaries between human and the spirit world to maintain balance and harmony with nature. With no medical facilities to care for the villages, the Bobohizans were often called to perform physical and spiritual healing.

With the high priest advice, a ritual called Moginakan was held. It was meant to seek the spirit of the astral realm and to ask for its intervention to protect the people.

As the days came nearer, the elders assembled all the villages young and old to assemble at the given spot, close to those who had died earlier.

Seven Bobohizans dressed in their custom ritual began to dance and chant, following the continued beating of the gong.

Seven Bobohizans doing the ritual dance.

The villages were in a state of awe and awaiting the contemplation of the spiritual response. The ritual continued for hours until the Bobohizans felt into a deep trance and began to dance uncontrollably and trembled as she made contact and reached out to the spirit world.

Moving On

An air of complete silence beheld on the tribes, as the Bobohizans were dancing to the end of their climax. Not even a pin drop could be heard. Among the crowd stood a young warrior named Monsompiad.

He was watching and waiting eagerly for the final spiritual words that were to come from the head of the Bobohizans.

As the ritual began to subside and the beating of the gong stopped, the Bobohizans began to speak in a frightening strident voice. The atmosphere surrounding the area was tense and ecstatic, as the Bobohizans began to speak.

Still in a trench, the Bobohizans spoke and breaking the silent atmosphere. The villagers listened in fear and gravely listening to what the spirit had instructed the villages to do.

The voice of the Bobohizans began to spell out clearly as their voice kept on cracking, stuttered with intensity as the instruction was given out to the villagers. They were told to build two rafts made of bamboo, strong enough to travel to an island far away.

Bamboo Raft similar to the request of the Bobohizans to carry the spirit from the island Journey to seek the spirit.

The journey had to be accompanied by thirty strong warriors and seven Bobohizans. During the journey, the Bobohizans had to chant continuously. They were accompanied by the beating of the gongs till they reached the island (Gaya Island). The spirit that the Bobohizans managed to reach out was presently staying on the island. Headed by Monsopiad, they reached the island without any untold incident. Guided by the Bobohizans, the thirty warriors headed to the various location in search of the dwelling place of the spirit.

The Bobohizans began to pray amidst the beating of the gong. They were searching the Monoliths as being prophesied by the priestess. It took them half a day to locate a huge stone by the side of the cliff. It was a big task as the stone was heavy and the other warriors were struggling and gasping heavily to move the stone to the bamboo raft.

The Bobohizans prayed and chanted to make the stone lighter so that it could be placed on the two rafts. The rest of the warriors were amazed at the strength of Monsompiad who could easily equal to several other warriors. They were not aware that Monsopiad got his inner strength given by the spirit of Bugan Bird.

The stone was placed on the raft and crossed the sea right up to the river close to Monsopiad village. It was pulled up to the river bank and dragged through the rice field to the hillock at Dazan.

The task was accompanied by the Bobohizans as the Warriors worked their way through. The ritual was followed by the sound of gongs, called the Pangkis at each step to ward off evil spirit. The Bobohizans chanted prayers continuously to summon the spirit to lighten their work. At their destination, the stone was erected on the site where they buried the plague victims.

The spiritual Gintutun's Megalith stood firmly in the ground

Moving On

An inauguration ceremony was held to appease the spirits family. Seven buffaloes, seven pigs, seven roasters and seven goats were slaughtered. The event lasted for seven days and seven nights amidst the chanting of the seven Bobohizans to inform the spirits their sanctuary had been erected firmly on the ground. The spirits are called GINTUTUN means "the ones who recognize and watch". From then on, Gintutun's duty is to protect the villages from any plaque and malice.

Ritual jars and gong located in the house of the skull

Monsopiad the renowned warrior continued with his task. With a group of his men, they prevented enemies from entering the village to steal their crops. He became well known throughout the land and none dare to cross his path.

Monsopiad had deep reverence with the spirit in the monolith. A bamboo platform was built in front of the monolith to place all the 42 skulls of his enemies to be shrunk. The Bobohizans were assigned to chant and protect the skulls before being brought to the house of skulls. In spite of his strength, Monsopiad did not live long.

Due to his fiery temper and rage, he had a quarrel with his neighbor and was injured. Finally, succumbing to the wound he incurred and died. However, the villagers erected a monument to honor the deeds he had done to the villages. Life continues in the village till this very day.

The padi barn

Joseph Jominol and the author trying their skill on the blowpipe at MONSOMPIAD Village Penampang

Relics of the past at Monsompiad village

EPISODE 12

Kampung Pogunon

Entrance to Kg Pogunon

Moving On

Kampung Pogunon at Penampang District

I met Lawrence Missi, a pensioner in Penampang and a deputy chairman of the Penampang District Coordinating Committee at a function. We had a short casual conversation to fill the time during one of the Penampang events. A few months later I met him again and promised to meet at one of the coffee shops in Penampang. After the short greeting and a coffee break, I went with him to his Kampong. We arrived at Kampong Pogunon about four kilometers from Penampang town. We were welcomed by an officer of Sabah Museum. He gave us a brief account of the various items on display with its legend prominently kept in the glass enclosure.

Ming Dynasty jar found in the vicinity of Kampung Pogunon

Ming dynasty artefact found at the site

We were then told all these items were excavated from the compound itself. A huge porcelain jar, some fragments of nineteenth Century Chinese blue and white bowls possible from Guangdong province in China. The jar and Fragments of human bones were nicely placed in a glass enclosed. The found items were fully accredited by a well-known anthropologist from Australia to verify its ethnicity and age.

Ming Dynasty porcelain found in the jar

Human remains found in the jar of the Ming period

About eight hundred years ago, most of the area here at Kampong Pogunon was the burial ground of the indigenous tribe. After a tour of the various items, we went out to the compound and visibly saw many Megalith firmly on its solid ground. Below the Megalith was either burial ground or put up to signify the rank of the buried person.

Megalith for Non- Inheritance individual

Megalith found in the vicinity of Kampung Pogunon

A round shape small Megalith signified a female and the bigger Megalith with the marking of lines showed the number of the heads the male warrior had killed.

The Megalith of a warrior, lines on the megalith showed number of heads killed.

I had visited three prominent landmarks of the Kadazan/Dusun spiritual grail of their tribe which correlated to the stories. I presumed these were the tribes that came to the land of North Borneo in the very early years of civilization.

Moving On

Commemorative Stone in Kampung Pogunon, Penampang district

Moving On

Kampung Pogunon in the forties

Lawrence Missi

Lawrence Missi has been living in this village for most of his life. He used to walk to schools with his other buddies. There were some flashing memories of his younger days that he could not forget.

I was somewhat curious and wanted to know more. He was somewhat reluctant but finally told me what had happened.

Lawrence and his friends were on the way home. Halfway, out came a tough guy. He was up to his mischiefs again to bully the kids as he used to do. He wanted to scare off the little kids just for the fun of it. In the past, these kids used to run for cover to escape from being bullied. As a result of this intimidation, they decided to walk in big groups. Out came the big guy, as usual trying to frighten off the young children. He would laugh like hell to watch the kids running into the padi fields like rabbits.

Fortunately, the children were prepared. They would not run as they were big in numbers. They decided to make a stand and confronted him face to face. They stood firm on their ground and waited for him to advance. The big tough guy took note of it but continued to approach the group. Moments later after receiving a few punches from the group of kids, he had to run up the hill and escape into the bushes. From that day onward, he dared not bother them. The big joker as mentioned above was Mr. Herman Luping, our former Tawau Youth Club advisor in 1965. He had just returned from overseas and was attached to the resident office as an administrative officer. Mr. Herman Luping was also the former Attorney General of Sabah. What a small world!

As we spoke further, another name that was familiar to me was mentioned. I was not aware that Mr. Nicholas Mok had moved to Kota Kinabalu from Tawau. He had spent some time in this kampong with some families. I knew him long ago when he was working as a plantation supervisor with Wing Yew Company. He was married to the daughter of a well-known timber and plantation merchant of Wing Yew Company. I had not seen him for many years since he left Tawau. According to James Dingon the museum officer, Nicholas spent most of his time planting medical herbs and stayed alone before he passed away.

The tragedy of love.

Whilst James and Lawrence were busy talking, I couldn't help but listen to some of the stories of lover's feud that ended in tragedy in this kampong.

It happened just after the war of 1945. This young man who came from the village Kg Tibabar Tambunan was madly in love with a young lass that he encountered in Kg Pogunon. His chemistry hit the center of his heart and could not forget her from that day onward.

He went to Kapayan and became a policeman. Being a policeman might get the respect of her father and the daughter. Unfortunately, he was late and came to know from friends that the girl was married to another guy and was currently pregnant. He was devastated and could not hold his emotion and desire. The love that he had for the girl kept on swirling about in his uncontrolled mind. Madly in love and couldn't control his passion. He began to plot out an evil deed. Being emotionally disturb, he drank until he got fully drunk. In a drunken rage mood, he went to the young lady's house at Kg Pogunon. He took out a spear and went straight to the girl's house. On the way, he killed six villagers and was calling out the girl to show herself to him. The lass kept herself indoor fearing for her life. He went under the house and pierced his spear through the floor to find the girl. Finally, he managed to kill the girl. The nearby neighbor saw the killing spree. He took his gun and shot him. He had only two bullets. One did not kill the guy until he rubbed the bullet with some sort of kitchen grime. As he laid dying, the man was hacked to pieces by the villagers. The priest came and gave the man a proper burial in spite of the carnage he had done.

The Jilted Lover

Another love case recorded in this kampong Pogunon was also about love which had no boundaries, the case of a jilted lover.

A beautiful lass by the name of Gampalung caught the attention of two guys. Both were trying to woo her. One guy came from Vugus or downstream of the Moyog River and the other guy was a local guy from the same Kampong with the girl. After months of competing to woo the beautiful lass, the Ketua kampong assembly the two guys and the girl. He asked the girl to choose between the two of them. The lass chose her kampong boyfriend instead. The other guy was badly hurt and had no intention to give her up. For several days he could neither sleep nor eat, as his mind had no other thought except the beautiful lass that he had lost. He decided to find ways and means to kill her quietly without causing any suspicion. Knowing that the girl walked the same path daily to feed her animals, the jilted lover placed some thorns spiked with poison along the footpath. She was found dead the next day and the villagers could not trace the cause of the girl's death.

EPISODE 13

The Penampang Hamlet

Joseph Jominol

Being a part of the pensioner association, I was able to meet Joseph Jominol, an easy going and kind at heart gentleman.

His father was the native chief of Penampang proper during the colonial days. Joseph has been staying in the kampong all his life. Joseph is willing to share with me his experience and interesting facts on the historical scenario of Penampang in the early part of the years after the Second World War.

Penampang was known as the stronghold of the Kadazan/Dusun people. Three hundred years ago before the influence of external culture, many of the kampongs were isolated. There were no proper roads except the footpath. It was a wild untamed village with head-hunters on the prowl. In the nineteen hundred, some external influence began and the tribes gradually began to tone down their earlier culture. To travel from one place to another or to seek medical help was a challenge, especially if one was in a dire situation and urgently needed a doctor. The patient normally died before reaching the hospital compound. The mood of travelling was mostly done on foot, bicycle or riding on buffaloes.

Their economy was based on agriculture and domestication of animals. The Dusun and Kadazan tribe continued to live a simple kampong life doing their normal daily chores of hunting, farming and looking after their domestic farm animals. Before the war as far back as in 1891, the population of North Borneo was only about sixty thousand. Probably many had perished due to a big flood that swept most of the South East Asian Continent in the year 1883.

This was due to the volcanic eruption that happened in Indonesia. There was a tsunami that flooded all low-lying areas. Whether it's a myth or not, a big flood destroyed most of the area along the coastal region of the country. Many parts of Penampang were low lying region except some hills and rock that protrude above the rest. The area was Kampung Hubah a Penampang proper. The surviving tribe managed to escape the flood by taking refuge at the "Pogun Savat rock". When the flood subsided, they returned to the kampong and called it Penampang.

The arrival of the Charted Company brought more advance migrants. With their know-how, changes to the kampong life in many sectors of the economy began to manifest. By this time the population had grown to about two hundred thousand and mix marriages were common in those days. Most of them were pagan and the pagan rite cultured thrive till this very day. Among the tribe stood a paramount leader, a leader selected by the chieftain of several villages. He is calling the Huguan Siou.

The Huguan Siou chief or the paramount ruler of the tribe had to be blessed by the spiritual elders of the Dusun Kadazan chief priest before he could adopt the name Huguan Siou.

With the coming of the missionaries and other migrants, the way of life of the indigenous people began to change. The hamlet once a serene and quiet place began to transform. The indigenous tribe began to feel the economic impact and many succeeded to upgrade their economic status.

Now Penampang has moved forward with many developments in the pipeline. The once scenic view of padi fields is drastically reduced.

In the year 2012, I went back to Penampang and tried to rekindle the former area that I visited. I found that the hamlet has completely transformed from a kampong scenario to a big town. Many amenities and facilities are made available. People are no longer living in huts and wooden house but a big bungalow and concrete houses. Several big malls can be seen along the highway. Many roads are built to provide access to most of the isolated villages.

Instead of buffaloes and footpath, vehicles of various types can be seen moving along the newly constructed trunk road.

Kampong Hubah

The Rock which derived the name of Penampang

Moving On

The name Penampang means rock, henceforth the name derived from a hill rock that saved the population from the great flood.

We could not dispel that the early Chinese that landed in Borneo were fishermen blown away from the South China Sea during the volcanic eruption, or even early warriors from China to seek fortune dispatched by the Ming Emperor.

Elders of the past at Kampung Hubah Standing from left1) ....2) Andrew Asing,3) Lee Kim Cheong,4) Lee Kim Hock 5) Lee Kim Chuan 6) ....7) ....8) Sitting (1) ....2) Sikayun 3) Jipiwing 4) Caroline Labangka (5) Maria Sugingging 6) Isdore Lee Bian Chu 7) Ingginon Basilik 8) Christina Jutan (9) Losingging 10) Lee Lian Soon 11) Lee So Na 12) Jacob Padasin 13) Sarah Lee Ke Soon 14) Dennis Luping

Standing L to R : Mataup , Pius Santani , Jacob Padasian , Isidore Lee Biansu , Lanjuat , Jugit
Sitting   L to R : Majawin , Bouniu , Mogunting , Mabagal , Asing , Junal .

The seniors in Kampong Hubah

Accompanied by Joseph Jominol, we visited the Kampung. I found many old houses still standing today. One such house was built in the year 1937. During the Japanese occupation in 1942, the house was used as the Japanese garrison. It was the same house that the allied knew the Japanese were occupying. The house was earmarked to be destroyed but failed. The mark of bullet holes is still visible. The owner leaves it untouched, as a reminder to the people of Penampang the horrors of war. The old lady, Madam Rose Bien Chu, the owner's daughter is still living there and is able to recollect some of the old tales.

Moving On

An old wooden house built in 1937 that was used by the Japanese as their garrison during the Second World War. This house belongs to Madam Rose Bien Chu

The house occupied by the Japanese during the Second World War. Marks of bullet holes can still be seen

The house at Kampung Hubah still occupied by the descendant.

The Catholic Church built its foundation in Kampong Hubah in the early nineties. It's propagated Christianity to the indigenous folks and many became Christian. The St Michael church was built of rock taken from the nearby hill.

The Penampang St Michael Church, the Christian Bastian Sabah North Borneo

St Michael Church in Penampang in 1965

The old boys of Penampang with Rev. Father Weber on 16 May 1939

As I was walking with Joseph Jominol, he had some war memories that he liked to share with me. He was staying in the same village with his parents and grandfather when suddenly he heard a knock on the door.

It was the Japanese soldiers that lived in one of the houses close to their kampongs. The Japanese knew that the village had plenty of food hidden in their barn and once a week took turns to confiscate rice and other requirements for their needs. Joseph Jominol was just about five years old, frightened, but stood his ground whilst holding tight to his mother.

He was surprised to see his uncle Alfonsiau Golunhu accompanying the Japanese soldiers to visit all the houses. Probably he had no choice but to follow the instruction of the Japanese administration. His uncle told the Japanese that this family was very poor. They couldn't even afford to buy a pair of pants for little Joe who stood there on his birthday suit. Seeing them with such pathetic look, the Japanese soldiers left and continued their rounds on other villages. The next day Joe had a bit surprised when the Japanese came and brought some pants for him to wear.

The iconic building at Penampang prefecture

As the war continuing unabated, the Japanese took a firm grip on the people. Properties were confiscated and many of the inhabitants suffered at the hands of the Japanese. The inhabitants were not allowed to move freely and the economic activities of the people were badly affected. As a result of these Japanese atrocities, an underground movement began to take shape in Inanam hamlet. It was headed by a young professional doctor, by the name of Albert Kwok. Albert was formally born in Kuching but came to North Borneo in the early years before the war. He started a movement called the Kinabalu Guerrillas. They made Inanam hamlet as their hideout and operation headquarters. With very little weapons, but a strong conviction, they began to galvanize the local villagers to join them. Prior to their plan of action, Albert met some allied forces from the Philippines and was given the assurance that some weapons would be provided. He had also conferred with some Suluk fighters from the Philippines who were willing to help him. The promises of the arms supply did not materialize and Albert was forced to continue the revolt with the men that he had and some available weapons such as shotguns, machetes and farming equipment.

The uprising caused Japanese casualties, and this action caused anger to the Japanese command. They instantly dispatched reinforcement from their headquarters in Kuching to quell the revolt. The reinforcement from Kuching enabled them to search the whole of Inanam hamlet and its surrounding. Fortunately, this intensive operation did not locate Albert Kwok. Whilst the Japanese were actively exploring the area, my uncle Paul Lai Kui Siong and his friends were in the vicinity of the jungle fringes collecting edible jungle plants. The Japanese saw them and wanted to detain them for interrogation. Fortunately, they managed to run and hide amongst the jungle corridor. It was indeed a close call. After the Japanese intensive operation, they still could not locate the guerrilla's whereabouts. To make the decisive onslaught on the final operation, the high command instructed the military commander to detain more than four hundred civilians, young and old from the Shantung village and gave Albert an ultimatum to surrender immediately or the civilian would be summarily executed. The news was relayed through an intermediary and reached the hidden secret location of the guerrillas. It was the moment of truth, as Albert and his men were put in a dilemma to adhere to the Japanese demand. Albert was given several days to make the biggest gamble of his life.

Finally, after giving some thought on compassionate ground, they surrendered. On 21 Jan 1944, Albert Kwok and his men were immediately executed in Petagas Putatan. Albert and his men gave their lives in exchange for four hundred of the Shantung populaces.

The Petagas memorial site where Albert Kwok and his men were massacred by the Japanese during World War 2

EPISODE 14

Awakening of Political Parties

After the formation of Malaysia, the populace of Sabah which was relatively small, began to galvanize into groups called parties. There were three main entities. Each representing the three-main ethnic group. USNO under Tun Mustapha representing the ethnic Muslim, Donald Stephen representing the Non-Muslim and the Chinese under SCA.

SCA had been known to inadvertently play the tipping scale when the two political parties closed neck to neck in an election. Donald Stephen party (UPKO) had the support of most of the Kadazan/Dusun party and the most vocal in the seat of Government. As the party became matured, some young men of the ethnic tribe stood above the rest.

The UPKO party in the sixties

The future leaders of tomorrow

One such young man that stood above the rest, came from the Penampang district at Kampong Hubah. Donald Peter Mojuntin was born on October 1939. As a young man, he started his career as a teacher in a primary school in 1958. He began his political interest in 1962 as the secretary general of UPKO. In 1963, he became a Member of Parliament. In 1967 he became a deputy in the legislative of Sabah. From 1972 to 1973, he became an Assistant Minister in the Industrial development. With the election of 1976 with Tun Fuad, he became the Minister of Municipal Administrator. Forty days later with several cabinet ministers, the plane crashed at Simbulan on 6 June1976.

In memory of those killed during the plane crash at Simbulan. Kota Kinabalu (double 6 tragedy)

It was the gloomiest day for the people of the state. A dramatic turn of event that changed the history of Sabah and the dynamic of the people.

Prior to the accident, there were several omens that transpired but was not foretold. Nancy, the wife of Peter had a dream before the plane crashed. She dreamt that she was in a church. The congregation was dress in black and were in a grief-stricken mood. She could not interpret the meaning of the dream, only to find out a week later that her husband had perished in a plane crash.

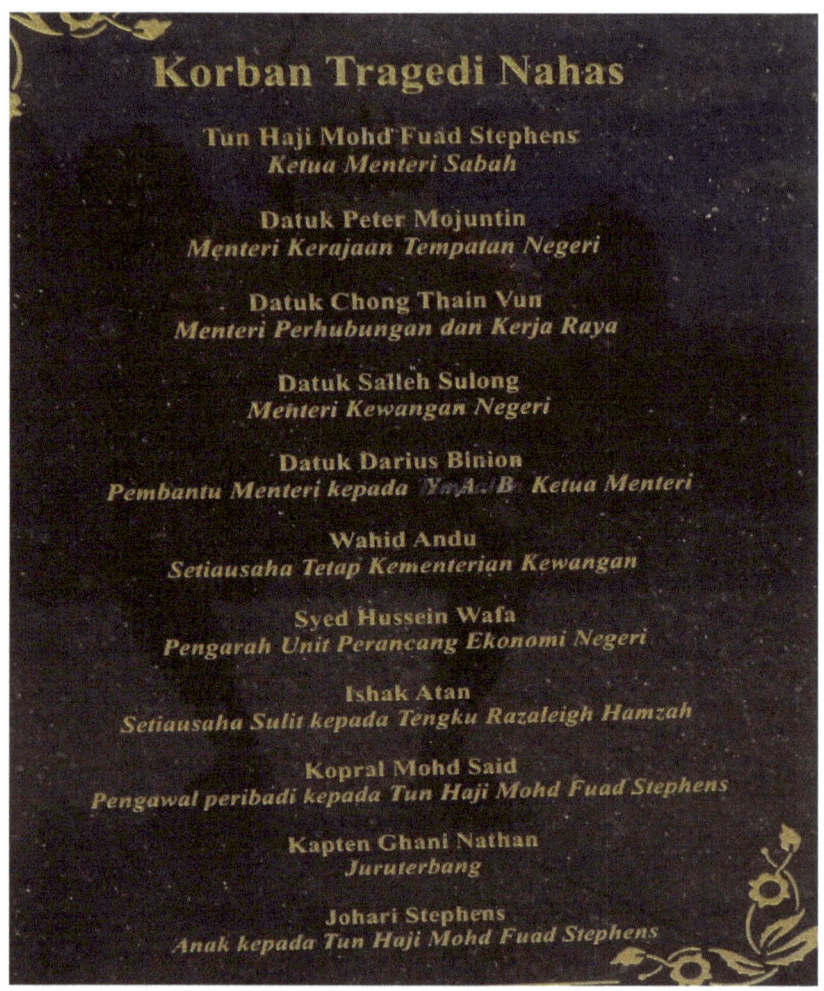

Those who perished at the crash site in Simbulan Kota Kinabalu Sabah

Moving On

Datuk Conrad Peter Mojuntin

Datin Nancy Mary Mojibon, a woman of great conviction, strong in her faith that kept her going. Courtesy of Datin Nancy Mojibon.

Besides the above premonition, something had also transpired in a friendly football match at the Penampang football field. They were competing for the Peter Mojuntin cup which was nicely laid on the table. The game was fiercely going on when suddenly a misguided ball hit the cup and dislodged the trophy from its casing and fell to the ground. In that instant, news came out that the plane from Labuan bringing the new Sabah cabinet ministers had plunged into the sea close to Simbulan area. Six cabinet members, including Peter Mojuntin, were on the plane. The public began to rush to the site and found that the plane had completely damaged beyond recognition. None of the passengers could have survived such an impact.

This event had a great bearing on the people of Penampang. The people of Sabah especially the Kadazan tribe were stunt and in a mood of disbelieve. A cloud of uncertainty emerged as the party began to take stock of its situation. New leaders began to unfold from their rank and the state, after such calamity managed to hold the bull by the horn.

The memorial site of Datuk Donald Peter Mojuntin in Penampang square

The legacy of Datuk Peter Mojuntin Kampung Hubah Penampang

EPISODE 15

My College Days

With the sound advice of Benjamin Kouju my former youth leader, I applied to enroll in the Gaya Teachers Training College in Jesselton. I began my course from 1967 and finished in 1968. Jesselton in those days were not fully developed. The road infrastructure was not as complex as now. Traffic jam was limited, only in certain areas.

On both sides of the road on the way to Penampang to Papar were padi fields and fruit trees as far as the eyes could see.

The legacy of the padi field in Penampang

The padi field area is gradually fading away

Moving On

All along the roads, fully clad indigenous women wearing round hats were busy cutting grass and cleaning the drainage around it. A scene we could find most areas of Kota Kinabalu and its surrounding areas.

My presence in Jesselton gave me the opportunity to visit several kampongs in the interior. The communities in the villages were down to earth friendly and full of hospitality. The village by itself had a picturesque beauty. As one entered the village, buffaloes and farmers could be seen everywhere. Some around the wet padlock, some fishing in the pond and several would be toiling in the field.

Buffaloes in the padi field at Penampang hamlet

Dongongon town in the sixties. The hamlet of Penampang

Women clad in their black attire, were busy on the rice field getting ready for the padi nursery. A traditional method handed down from generation to generation. Animals such as dogs, pigs, chicken and ducks were roaming in the vicinity of the house.

On my returned to Kota Kinabalu in the year 2007.the whole area has transformed after more than forty years. More roads were built connecting villages and towns. The Penampang district has developed into a metropolitan town, with malls and concrete houses everywhere.

The new urban, replacing the old Dongongon town.

Entrance to the Kadazan/Dusun Cultural Centre

The Kadazan/Dusun Cultural Centre

The new mall in Jalan Penampang

The second Kadazan/Dusun Cultural Centre.

The Penampang Chinese Temple in the center of town

EPISODE 16

The enterprising city of Kota Kinabalu

After having settled in Kota Kinabalu quite comfortably, my mind began to recap my former town. Thinking of the good old days I used to have in Tawau.

Questions began to pop up in my mind, whether I had made the right decision to have left Tawau. Probably I had, but circumstance lead one thing to another.

The visit by members of the executive committee of PPKS from Kota Kinabalu started the ball rolling. Coincidently, I was in the right place and time to meet several executive members of the pensioner association. The close rapport led to one thing to another that propelled me into their fraternity. Since then I have been fully committed to the activities of the association.

After staying in Kota Kinabalu for more than a year, my attachment to Tawau gradually fades away.

I need to remind myself that I am no longer a stranger here, but a prodigal son after having lost in the wilderness.

To recap for a while, I had to remind myself that I was in Jesselton in 1947 with my parents, when the town was made the administrative centre of North Borneo.

Both my wife and I settled quite comfortably in my daughter's Home at Luyang Perdana.

To stay home and watch television was not my piece of cake. So I decided to make time more pliable by visiting several interesting places that Kota Kinabalu had to offer. I was captivated by the many recreational places the government of the day had built.

The tall building of Yayasan Sabah and many high rise upper-end condo units stand proudly with a scenic view of the islands around it.

Kota Kinabalu has much to offer in terms of facilities and recreational areas.

I am glad I did the right thing to return to this ancestral village of my clan.

Although my clan had started their lives in Kota Kinabalu in the early part of North Borneo, I had no idea of their existence. My parents never told us about it.

It was due to this void, which enticed me to dig further and search the rest of my family clan living in Kota Kinabalu and other parts of towns in Sabah.

I heard many have gone overseas searching for greener pasture. With the extensive advancement in communication, I am sure that the link could be made to relatives currently residing in many parts of the world.

Kota Kinabalu has now developed into a cosmopolitan city with its own mayor. It's the seat of the current government. Most government building has been upgraded. The road infrastructure has also being built to accommodate the ever increasing population needs. The mammoth road link between Sabah, Brunei and Sarawak has begun.

Moving On

A new scenic view of the Sabah Government Administrative building

The new Court House in Kota Kinabalu Sabah

Second opinion

I have some problem with my vision, so I decided to get second opinion to seek modern method in cell therapy. With some advice from my children, I took a trip to Singapore. We went to the most advance eye clinic in the country.

Regrettably, the expectation I had, have not yet reach the shore of Singapore. The best remedy they could do in Singapore was to put an artificial cornea. The prospect of failures was greater and I could not take any chances. I then went to the eye specialist at Sungai Besi hospital Kuala Lumpur and got the same answer. My final bet was in Petaling Jaya but also got the same finding. In Petaling Jaya, I got one of my cataracts removed and after the operation, the thick glass that had caused so much inconvenience to me was discarded. It was a great relief to me to wear thinner eyeglasses.

As I have mentioned earlier, I was in Petaling Jaya for an eye operation. During the waiting period, I met a total stranger at the clinic. He was a retired gentleman waiting for his turn to see the eye specialist. As usual, from a smile, salutation came the conversation.

After the preview, we were just about to leave when the gentleman called us. He offered us a room in his house. I was taken aback for a while and did not give him an immediate response. My wife and I felt it was not nice to impose on others or to take advantage of someone generosity.

We respectfully and sincerely declined. He kept on insisting and after constant persistence, we accepted his kind hospitality. We then followed him home in Petaling Jaya.

We stayed for a week and went out with him often. The couples were very kind and made us feel at home.

We stayed for a week before flying back to Sabah. We thanked him for his kind generosity and wanted to reimburse his expenses on food. He flatly refused to accept. What an unexpected warm experience that we had gone through. As the saying goes, "a good deed is always rewarded with a reciprocal karma". This kind gentleman reminded us that kindness still exists in this part of the world.

Catching up on computer courses

We returned to Kota Kinabalu after my eye odyssey

I began to spend time on my computer screen, only to find that the function had retreated. Probably it needed a long rest after years of service in Tawau. I had no choice, but to dig into my wallet, and get a new advanced computer.

In this modern age, computer is a must in every able bodied person. WITHOUT IT is like losing your brain and lost to the whole wide world.

This newly found modern technology has opened the window of opportunity to the wider world. Offhand information is always available at our fingertip. The data is tremendous and the sky is the limit.

The government of the day has given ample opportunity for pensioners to learn the skill.

Computer Course for PPKS Members

PPKS members to enhance their computer skill

Seniors learning modem gadget at Beringis Resort Kota Kinabalu

Pensioners learning the skill to monitor their health through the use of a smartphone. Brian Bong the specialist was there to help them.

EPISODE 17

My close relative

Ricky Azcona

Ricky my cousin is the only cousin that I have close rapport with. Ricky and I had a long story since young. We were born in the same year in Sandakan. His mother and my mother were sisters. We stayed in the same place at kampong Gulam. Our mothers were having a hard time bringing us up during the Second World War in Sandakan.

After staying several month in Kota Kinabalu, I began to enquire his whereabouts and to try and make the necessary contacts. Fortunately, after months of search, I was able to meet him. I managed to acquire some of my relative's whereabouts and contacted them. From that day onward, both of us were busy putting the puzzle in place of all our relatives in Kota Kinabalu.

Both Ricky's father and mine had a very interesting wartime stories. They were both involved in the underground movement. Ricky's father provided vital information on Japanese location to the allied and my father provided medical aids to the Australian prisoners of war.

As a result of their clandestine operation, both were detained by the Japanese kampitai.

They were sent to Kuching as prisoners of war. Ricky's father did not return as he was condemned to death by the Japanese court. My father returned when the war was over.

After the war in 1945 my dad continued his service in the civil hospital. At the end of 1946, he was assigned to the dispensary in Tongod Kinabatangan. From Sandakan, we went upstream through the Kinabatangan River using a sampan. It took us one week to arrive in the village.

From that day onward, I did not meet Ricky until 1953, the year I was sent to St Mary's School in Sandakan.

Ricky's family and I stayed with the Delgado family, my grandmother's brother. The house had limited rooms, but the Delgado family was very accommodating, the marking of a Pilipino culture.

We slept in any spare corner of the house. Just a simple mat, a pillow and something to cover us were our normal sleeping area. During the day, the beddings would be kept under the table or elsewhere.

When Ricky's family moved to another house, I followed them. I was ten years old. From our kampong, we had to walk to school. We passed through a Chinese school and graveyard. As we climbed up the hill, we passed through several bombed craters before reaching our destination.

After more than forty years, Ricky and I finally met in Kota Kinabalu in 2010. I was told he wanted to migrate to the Philippines with his family and sold everything he had. He stayed in the Philippines for several years.

The house that he had in the Philippine was within the range of some active volcanoes. It was a town rich in culture, fertile soil and beautiful scenery.

The family had settled comfortably and the children were schooling happily. Then without warning the volcano began to erupt. Many were evacuated including Ricky's family. In a show of force, it erupted and destroyed everything on its way. The family lost everything and Ricky decided to move back to Sabah.

In spite of all the misfortune he encountered, he kept his head high and tried to make the best of life that he still had.

In Kota Kinabalu, Ricky and I spent our free time meeting and getting to know other family members whom I have lost touch.

In the year 2016, he travelled to the Philippines using the rat trail from Sandakan. He succeeded in reaching the Philippines and archived his goal of meeting someone important. I did not inquire the purpose of his visit, as this was his personal matter.

During the journey, the boat was stopped by the police and military on the high seas. They managed to pass, due to the power of "money is king".

The moment of tribulation

Ricky gave me an insight into the years his mother had suffered, due to the Japanese occupation

The Azcona family in Sandakan before the Second World War

Before the war

Prior to the Second World War, Ricarte's grandfather Manuel wanted to leave Miri and return to the Philippines with his family. They had to go through Labuan. However, all shipping vessels to the Philippines were stopped. Mr. Manuel decided to move his family to Sandakan as it was closer to Zamboanga in the Philippines. At that moment, the Japanese had already landed in Sandakan. Mr. Manuel then decided to stay put and settled in Sandakan with his family, pending the end of the war.

He had so many children to care for and no definite disposable income. It was fortunate that he had some savings from his previous job in Sarawak which was just enough for him to invest in a small plot of land.. Manuel was formerly working for an oil company in Sarawak. He had vast experience in the mechanical field

The said land was situated at mile 23 Labuk road. It was big enough to build his family house and other uses to temporarily sustain his family's needs.

Manuel was indeed lucky to have bought the property. Adjacent to his land was a property belonged to a Dutch company.

The Dutch company that owned the land nearby had invested a large sum of money to plant rubber trees.

His purchase of the land came at the right time. He decided to take a temporary job with the Dutch company called Sandakan Estate

The estate had a manager by the name of John Funk and estate supervisor, Mr. Chong.

During the tenure of their work, Manuel and the two men began to foster an understanding of one another and became good buddies.

They spent much of their free time discussing the on-going war and the occupation of Sandakan by the Japanese military. Occasionally they would touch on the fate of the allied prisoners. It was common knowledge among the people of Sandakan that the Prisoners of war were inhumanly treated. They were forced to work at the newly constructed airfield. The prisoners were not given proper meal and medical attention.

During their holidays, Mr. Chong and Manuel would venture into the Sipuluk forest to hunt for wild animals. Quite often, they would bring home chunks of meat for the family and workers on the estate. There were no shortages of food, especially meat. However, the Japanese on a certain instance would demand some wild meat. They had no choice but to accede to their request.

Sandakan under Japanese occupation

When the Japanese entered Sandakan, the British officers stationed in Sandakan had left, knowing that resistance would be hopeless. Only essential personnel such as doctors and other critical requirements were left to continue their service.

The Japanese were trying hard to win the hearts and minds of the local people. In the midst of their pursuit to pacify, a local captain of the Japanese garrison had a very close rapport with the Azconas.

The Azconas were musically inclined and so was the Japanese captain. It was this interest and love of music that bonded them together. This friendship formed a new beginning that would become an asset in the later part of the war.

Manuel was a good guitarist and loved to sing. His wife Remeja was a reserved and conservative lady.

Among all his sons, Felix seemed to acquire the greatest talent in the musical field. It was his love of music and songs that he met Tasciana Lobos, the daughter of Ambrossa Valentino Lobos. Their encounter gradually bloomed into love.

Felix and Taciana

It wasn't too long before Felix decided to approach his parents. Calmly, he requested his father's blessing to marry the girl that he adored. To his surprise, the answer given was negative. He was devastated and came as a shock. He never expected his father would reject him. Furthermore, he warned him not to meet or have any further contact with Tasciana. He gave no reasons for his objection. Felix was emotionally disturbed by his parent's rebuke. He determined to continue the relationship, in spite of his father's objection.

In a state of mental and emotional anguish, he continued to meet Tasciana in secret. The secret rendezvous brought some relief to him. Besides his normal day to day work, Felix would give piano lessons in the evening. One of his pupils was a little girl called Elizabeth. He would ask her to pass his love letters to Tasiana and vice versa. Elizabeth was happy to do his bidding as she would always get a reward for it.

Finally, Felix could not wait any longer. He approached his parents the second time. He was flatly snubbed. In his desperate situation, he contemplated suicide. Fortunately, he came to his senses in time. Felix then decided to elope and marry Tasciana instead. So, he left the comfort of his parents' home to pursue the girl of his dreams.

They got married at Tasciana's family home in Lupak Mualas. His family was not present during his marriage to Tasciana. Since then, Felix has kept his distance from his family and did not even make any visit to his mother or siblings. This contentious issue lasted for several months until the time when Felix was arrested by the Japanese.

The Sandakan Chinese

Due to the invasion and occupation of China, the Chinese in Sandakan had the great distrust of the Japanese. The Chinese community had been contributing large sums of money to their motherland.

When the Japanese knew about the Sandakan Chinese providing aid to China, they were constantly under watch by the Kampitai. This constant inspection and harassment affected their business and livelihood. Some were arrested, tortured and killed.

With the ongoing intimidation by the Japanese administration, some of the Chinese community began to plot to overthrow the Japanese occupation.

The underground Cell

Mr. John Funk had secretly formed an alliance with the American by way of radio communication code-named LB2 (Labuk Boys). He met Felix, the son of his good friend Manuel. Felix was working as a surveyor at that time and was well-versed with the terrains around Sandakan. This skill was much needed by the alliance, so he decided to recruit him to join them in the underground activities.

John briefed Felix on his involvement in the underground and the work that they had carried out. He told him that they needed his help in the clandestine affair. However, he was very cautious not to pass any information of importance that might jeopardize their operation in case Felix did not agree to his proposal.

Felix was put in dithering situation. He had to respond to John's request quickly. He was thinking of his wife and child-to-be. Tasciana at that time was pregnant with the first child. After much thought, he finally accepted John's request.

John was pleased when Felix agreed to offer his service to their course. After Felix was recruited, his first task was to get information on the Japanese movement, infrastructure and their logistic. A task tantamount to acting as a spy.

He travelled as far as Telupid and Beluran Kalagen to get the exact location of the Japanese campsite. This important information was relayed by radio code to the Americans stationed in the Philippines. In 1942, just after the New Year, the allies began their bombing mission.

The trepidation periods

The Japanese were mystified at the accuracy of the bombers in targeting their vital location. They began to be suspicious and acted. Finally, they managed to trace the source and the activities of the LB2. Some of the members were rounded up but a few managed to evade them. Those arrested were sent to the Japanese prison camp situated at mile 7, Labuk Road.

Fortunately for the Azcona family, the Japanese captain who had befriended them earlier would warn them of an impending search and urge them to hide in the jungle. Remeja Abad was forced to drag her children into the jungle around Sungai Manila. They hid in the jungle for days and weeks to evade the Japanese. It was indeed torturous for the family, especially when food and water were scarce.

It was only when the soldiers had given up the search area and returned to their barracks that their Japanese captain friend would signal them that the coast was clear and safe enough to return home.

The Mysterious Disappearance of Manuel Azcona (Ricarte's grandfather)

Mr. Manuel Azcona

Meanwhile, Manuel who had been working for the Dutch Company was assigned by the Japanese to work in their workshop. His job was to maintain the military vehicles in their possession. Secretly, he began to sabotage the Japanese mode of transport and other equipment. His action caused much inconvenience to the Japanese authorities with the constant breakdown of their vehicles and machinery. At first, the Japanese did not suspect anything, but as more vehicles were needed to overhaul due to engine failure, they suspected something was amiss.

Manual was suspected but they had not got any solid proof of his misconduct. However, he was put under their observation. They wanted to arrest him but would wait until they could prove that he was the saboteur.

On December 1942, a week before Christmas, Manuel and his good friend Mr. Chong decided to venture into the jungle for their usual hunting activity. Since Christmas was just around the corner, it would be a bonus if they could get some wild boar meat for the Christmas celebration.

They went into the jungle at Sepuluk in Sungai Manila. The next day, Mr. Chong returned alone to the plantation. Manuel was not with him. He claimed that he did not see him after their hunting trip. Manual's wife,

Remeja was waiting eagerly for him to return the next day. With the hope that he would be bringing home some meat for Christmas. She waited in vain. Several days passed by and Manuel had not returned.

Remeja became more frantic with worry but dared not report his disappearance to the Japanese Police. It was quite common and normal in those days for people to disappear without any trace. They were either secretly being arrested by the Japanese or simply disappeared. Besides, there was speculation that Manuel might have been arrested by the Japanese. The family was kept in the dark about his whereabouts until after the war ended.

Remeja Abad (The Iron Lady)

With Manuel missing, Remeja had the arduous task of bringing up the children all by herself. It was indeed a very tough life, especially with the war going on. She had to face events and the ordeal that had marred her life. With the loss of her husband, the breadwinner, she faced an uncertain future. Her situation was made worse when her house on the estate, the only sanctuary that she could depend on, was completely razed to the ground by the Japanese army. This was most probably done in response to Felix's involvement with the anti-Japanese activities.

Moving On

Felix Azcona

In the beginning, Felix was able to elude the Japanese who were constantly on his heels. He had to go into hiding and was constantly worried about his wife Tasciana and his only son Ricarte, or Ricky as he was fondly called.

On one occasion, Tasciana's father was gravely ill, so she decided to pay him a visit. There were no other means to travel except on foot, but somebody had to accompany her to reach her father's house which was about fifteen miles away. Felix had no choice but to contact his family for help.

Felix appealed to his brother, Reggie, to assist them. After much persuasion, Reggie agreed but albeit reluctantly. Throughout the journey, Tasciana had to carry her son Ricky who was only a few months old.

Along the way, her arms grew tired and she had hoped that Reggie would lend a hand to reduce her burden just for a while. Reggie ignored her, and continued to walk without feeling any sympathy for his sister-in-law. When they finally reached Lupak Meluas in the evening, Tascina almost collapsed due to exhaustion and she felt excruciating pain throughout her whole body. This incident showed that Felix's family still blamed her for 'enticing' him away from them.

The search for Felix Azcona

The Japanese were high on the heels of the underground members, especially Felix. Finally, the Japanese took a drastic course of action, by putting words out to the families and local populace that they would face fatal consequences if found hiding Felix in their midst.

Felix was in a fix and a dilemma. He knew that the Japanese would always carry out their threats as they had made in China. Felix had to consider all the options within his means. Finally, after exhausting every viable option, he decided to surrender for the sake of his family.

His mother and sibling who had gone hiding because of him, came out when words came to them that it was safe for them to return to their home. However, upon their arrival, they were horrified to see that their house had been burnt to the ground. The Funk family kindly allowed them to stay at their storehouse.

Remeja then heard that her son had been detained by the Japanese Police and interned at the prison camp at mile 7. Remeja was able to get permission to visit her son at the camp. During the visit, he instructed her to gather all the important documents kept at the house. He was not aware that their house had been razed to the ground by the Japanese. Remeja did not have the heart to tell him of their situation. Felix and the rest of the prisoners were then sent to the Berhala Island before they were shipped to Kuching.

In Kuching, they were brought before a Military Court. Felix was found guilty of spying and sentenced to death.

The Japanese Surrender

In 1945, just before Christmas, the Japanese surrendered and withdrew from Sandakan town. Remeja, who was throughout that time in the dark of her son's whereabouts, decided to go to the detention center to search for Felix. She was not aware that Felix was sent to Kuching two years ago. Distressed and disappointed, she could only suffer silently. It was later that she found out Felix had been executed by the Japanese and buried in Kuching. Meanwhile, Tasciana had been accepted by the family and was then staying with them.

Moving On

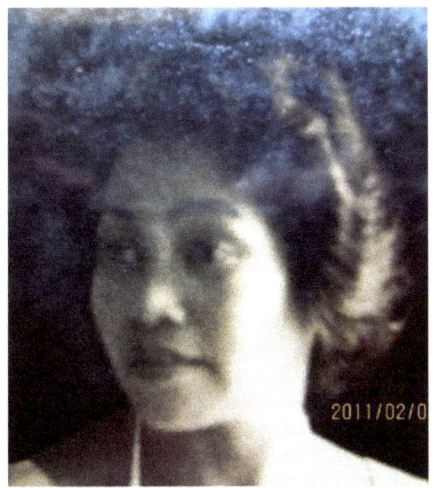

Tasciana Villealobos, wife of Felix Azcona

Taciana at the Kuching Memorial in Sarawak

The Confession (1945)

In 1945, after the war ended, Remeja was surprised that her husband's hunting-buddy, Mr. Chong, paid her a visit. He was suffering from a fatal illness and had not much time to live. So, he decided to confess to Remeja, a burden that he had been carrying throughout the years. In a regrettable voice, he confessed to her the true nature of her husband's disappearance.

He recalled on that fateful day before Christmas, both of them had decided to hunt for wild boars in the jungle. Armed with shotguns, they split up to hunt in different areas of the jungle.

After an hour of walking, Mr. Chong decided to climb a tree and waited for the boar. After a while, he heard some noise coming out in his direction. Without hesitation, he shot. Only to find that the object he shot, was Mr. Manuel and not the wild boar he expected.

In a spur moment of shock and panic, he hurriedly left him dying there and hid in the plantation.

Remeja was shocked and appalled by the confession. It horrified her to think that this man, her husband's best friend, could actually leave him in the jungle to die. She calmly controlled her temper and composure, looked at the man in the eyes and said, "Thank you, now you may leave the house!" This revelation prompted the family to search for his remains, to give him a proper Christian burial. After a thorough search, they could not find any trace of Manuel.

After the war, Remeja remained in Sandakan with her two daughters and son Conrad @ Franco. The rest of her children had left for other towns in Sabah.

Later, Remeja was able to contact her brother-in-law, Arthur Azcona, in Seria Brunei. He invited her to Brunei, an offer which she gladly accepted. She stayed with him for two years trying to erase all the traumatic period of her life during the Second World War.

Two years later, she decided to move back to Sandakan and stayed with her brother Peter Abad at his house near to the Town Padang. In 1953, the house was torn down and they moved away to another part of the town. Remeja stayed in Sandakan until her death.

EPISODE 18

The Sacred Heart Alpha community

The Sacred Heart Senior Alpha group 2016 in Kota Kinabalu Sabah

Adrian Majaham

On my first few months in Kota Kinabalu, Adrian Majaham had been a good buddy. He brought me around Kota Kinabalu town in his car, showing the various places of interest.

Through his wide range of contacts, we managed to meet several old friends.

We went to the senior citizen Club, hoping to meet some pals. The secretary brought us around to show the various facilities made available to seniors. After the visit, both us joined as members. Adrian also took the liberty to join the Sabah Government Pensioners Association and was nominated as the assistant secretary. After a year, Adrian preferred the spiritual aspect of his life and spent his time in the Alpha movement of the Sacred Heart Cathedral.

Adrian incessantly invited me to join the Alpha group "COME AND SEE", he said. I took note of it and waiting for a good day when my disposition urged me to take the path to the church compound.

Then one early morning, I decided to respond to Adrian's call and went to the function. At the function, I met some of my old friends and in particular a guy by the name of Henry Shim who was my classmate at St Mary's Primary School in 1953. I could not have recognized him until he mentioned that both of us were in the same school and class.

Moving On

Henry Shim and the author.

Henry was originally from Tawau, a well knows Shim's clan. His mother was a nurse and his father were one of the seven who were killed by the Japanese in Tawau during the occupation. He was arrested because of his membership in the secret society to collect fund for China's cause. After the war, Mrs. Shim was reemployed by the British and served in Sandakan Civil Hospital. Her son Henry was sent to St. Mary School in 1953. Both of us were in the same class.

I left Sandakan in 1954 and back at Holy Trinity School Tawau. Henry's aunt was my teacher whom I fondly called her teacher Lucy. She was kind and very conscientious in her work. I was rebellious in class, but she managed to pacify me.

During my stay in Kota Kinabalu, I heard she was staying along the Luyang housing estate. I needed to find her, no matter how long it would take. Fortunately, by the grace of God, I was able to locate her house after a long search. Without any reservation, I paid her a surprise visit. She had a maid who at first hesitant to let me in.

After more than sixty years, I finally met the teacher who had given me the meaning of love and patience. Unfortunately, she was blind, very sickly and laid on the bed.

I called her name and spoke to her. She could immediately recognize my voice in spite of her situation. She stretched her hand to feel my face as I was holding the other hand tightly. There were tears in her eyes as she recollected those days in 1956 in Tawau during Father Bekama's time. She was so happy to know that one of her old pupils from primary one in Holy Trinity School Tawau had come to see her. I prayed for her recovery though knowing that she had very little time left. Several months later I heard she had gone to the Lord and finally rest in peace.

I continue to participate in the Alpha event. A casual meeting for seniors to inculcate better bond. It also provides us with a window of opportunity to make new friends. I was delighted to be welcomed by the virtuous people during my first visit. The event began with a good breakfast, followed by a film show. It ended with group discussion. Members were free to leave at any time without compulsion. My first visit attracted my interest and since then I have been going without fail.

Alpha yearly activities. The jolly good guys
Madam Quirine, Anthony Lim and wife

The Sacred Heart Alpha Group was started by a dedicated conscientious Catholic group. It is under the leadership and pioneers of Daniel Kong, Mr. Anthony Lim and other parishioners. It is held every Tuesday morning and outdoor activities at year end.

Sacred Heart Alpha motivational talk

Alpha activities accompanied by the live musical band

Alpha seniors singing with joy.

Getting together by some senior Alpha's group

The cell group of Sacred Heart Alpha from Left: Francis Wong, Peter Siburat, Timothy Wong, Daniel Chan, Bryan Paul Lai, James Dusti, Ronald Leong, Michael Wong and Adrian Majaham the cell leader

EPISODE 19

Doreen Hurst helping hand

Doreen Hurst, the lady that I met in Sandakan six years ago managed to communicate with me through the email. She told me that the money she promised six years ago was forthcoming.

The book that she wrote had gone on sale. With some of the profit made, she would send the money as soon as possible. She asked me to distribute the money back to the folks along the death March route from Sandakan to Ranau.

It was beyond my expectation, for her to keep the end of the bargain. I was somewhat flattered by her trust, in spite of us meeting only once.

I accepted her offer and promised to abide by her request. On the other hand, how am I going to do it? Issue such as this had to be done in a proper and transparent manner. I could not act alone. I needed a committee or several associates to handle the job.

After giving some thoughts, I decided to invite several of my close friends in the pensioner committee.

The following persons came across my mind; Datuk Thomas V.E. Majinal, Mr. Joseph Jominol, Fred Morris Sepajil, Adrian Dominic @ Majahan and Aloysius Bungkilan. These were the members that I felt would be amicable to lend me their helping hand.

After presenting my suggestion, they accepted to be part of the committee. Our first informal meeting was held in a well-known coffee shop called Kedai Sin Hin in Dongonen town.

The Doreen Funk Welfare Committee formed to cater the needs of the poor along the death march in Ranau from left: Fred Morris, Bryan Paul Lai, Datuk Thomas M. Joseph Jominol and Aloysius Bungkilan

At the preliminary meeting, a committee was formed and Datuk Thomas was duly nominated as the chairman.

During our dialogue, Datuk Thomas presented his views. He was somewhat concerned that this project of providing aid might give some wrong impression to certain political parties.

The committee took note of Datuk Thomas remarks. The committee had to ensure not to raise the public's eyebrow and misunderstood by any party as political in nature. We needed to ensure all activities had to be run on a low-key basis.

The request to disperse along the death March route had to be defined clearly. The death March route as suggested had nowhere to be seen after more than fifty years.

The chairman then requested to know whether the poor in Penampang area could be considered. The said question would be referred to Doreen Hurst for her final conclusion.

On our subsequent meeting, the committee was informed that the matter raised by Datuk Thomas had now been approved by the donor.

Several villages in the Penampang district were located, endorsed and agreed by the committee. They were kampong Bunduon, Kampong Hubah, Kampong Tunoh Hungap, Kampong Penapah Kondis, Sugud and Timpangoh.

Our schedule was laid out to visit the villages. Before we proceeded, the committee bought all the essential goods such as rice, sugar, salt coffee, flour and other necessities, After the Penampang hamlet, we proceeded on to Paginatan Ranau.

Hamlet of Paginatan Ranau

The Doreen Hurst Welfare Fund Committee. From left Joseph Jominol Fred Morris Datuk Thomas and Bryan Paul Lai the author. Not present Adrian Majaham and Aloysius Bungkilan

Paginatan is about forty kilometers from Ranau Township. It's about the same distance to Telupid District. This was the route where more than two thousand allied forces mostly Australian experienced the horrible death march to Ranau in 1945.

The members left Kota Kinabalu to Ranau around 7.30 am by Land Cruiser. Those members included Datuk Thomas Majanil, Bryan Paul Lai, Joseph Jominol, Fred Morris Sipaji and Walter our joyful skipper/driver.

From left: Andrew Koinod, Datuk Thomas Majinal, Joseph Jominol, Aloysius Labi and Bryan Paul Lai. Sitting on the stone: Fred Morris Sepaji

The committee stopped for a while at a small tuck-shop to purchase all the necessary supplies such as rice, cooking oil, sugar, coffee powder and salt. We reached Ranau town around noontime and joined by the Ranau coordinator Mr. Aloysius Labi and Mr. Andrew Koinod.

After lunch at Ranau town, we proceeded to kampong Paginatan and arrived at the Health Clinic at 1.30 p.m.

The Paginatan Health Clinic

Morris trying to get some information from the villagers

We were warmly welcomed by the family of Matius Gawanti whose wife was related to Domiman Bt OKK Akui who took care of some Australian soldiers by hiding them in the jungle of Paginatan at great risk.

Mr. Matius Gawanti led us to the village community centre of Kg Paginatan. We were introduced to Mr. Jaimin Alexius Geoffrey (Chairman Village Operator Council-Daya Wawasan Gerakan Desa cum Chairman Farmers Association. Kinabalu /Paginatan), Mr. Albert Souting (Village headman), Ketua Kampong Mr. Pius Korop (Chairman Security, health and development committee-JKKK). There were about fifty villagers including children were present at the community centre.

Mr. Aloysius Labi made a short speech to introduce the rest of the committee. Datuk Thomas welcomed the villagers and gave a short account of the donor Doreen Hurst. He spoke a short history of Doreen Hurst background, and her effort to depict the local's sacrifice during the Second World War. She had written a book portraying the harrows of Japanese atrocities to the Sabahan.

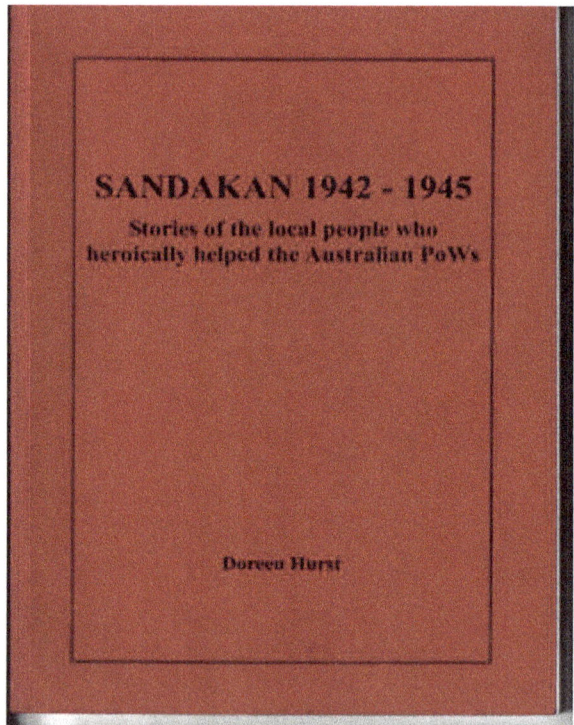

The book written by Doreen Hurst

She also wrote about the tribe of Paginatan who helped the Australia soldiers.

As a token of appreciation to these villagers, she had contributed some money to buy some rations for them. The head man, in return, thanked the committee for the kind donation.

Discussion with the Ketua Kampung before the ration is given out

The villagers thanked the Doreen Hurst Committee for the donation

The villagers with the committee

The ration that cost about Malaysian Ringgit
three thousand were distributed

Moving On

The discussion took quite a while to explain the purpose
of the donation and where it came from.

Datuk Thomas handling out to the first recipient

Andrew Koinod distributing a bag of rice and other essentials

Mr. Fred Morris handing out ration to the kampong folks

Several momentous left by the Australian visitors who went to the village.

Before returning to Kota Kinabalu, we went to Tagal Sigai Moroli Kg Barcxh to dip ourselves in the river for fish therapy. A well-known site for tourist in the district. The committee thanked the Ranau coordinator for their help and safety drove back to Kota Kinabalu.

ROMA LITTLE GOAT DONATION

Back in Kota Kinabalu, I received an email from Doreen that she would be crediting my account with another one thousand Australian dollars from an old lady by the name of Roma Little.

The money donated was the purpose of purchasing several goats to present it to any poor villagers along the death March route. The committee once again faced with a predicament. A task which was beyond our skill. It took us several weeks and several meetings to discuss the right way to solve the matter.

The chairman Datuk Thomas suggested to the committee to acquire the goats. Mr. Morris was appointed to build a small pen to keep the goats temporary.

The committee gave some fund for Fred Morris to build a small hut near to his house.

A few months later several of the goats gave birth, but due to the constricted temporary hut, the kids died. Finally, we had no choice but to send the goats to one of the missions in Sook. Thus, the end of Fred Morris responsibility to care for the animals.

The balance of the money kept was credited to the Catholic Church in Sandakan and the committee dissolved.

EPISODE 20

Nunuk Ragang Chamber

In 2016, the Sandakan Municipal Council extended another invitation. I was asked to attend the War Memorial Ceremony to read a short poem written by Bill Young, the Australian prisoner of war during the second world war of 1941-1945.

I drove all the way from Kota Kinabalu accompanied by Ricky. Along the way, we stopped at a well-known highly spiritual iconic building of the Kadazan/Dusun tribe called Nunuk Ragang. A monument which stood proudly by the side of the Labuk River Bank.

The entrance to Nunuk Ragang chamber

The memorial site was built in 2004. The historical text found at

Nunuk Ragang or call the Red Ficus tree

Ricky Azcona looking at the red ficus tree

The tree that stood adjacent to the building had played a significant role to understand the origin of the indigenous people of Sabah.

The site was located near a village called Tampias. Nunuk refers to the banyan tree and Ragang short form Aragang means red color. The monument was used by the Kadazan/Dusun tribe as a spiritual inauguration ceremony of the

Paramount chief called the Huguan Siou. The ritual is performed by the priestess or Bobohizans to install the paramount leader of the Kadazan /Dusun tribe.

The ritual has been going on for a decade and it is one of a unique ritual performed by the tribe. Without the ritual, the

Huguan Siau would not be given the accredited position.

The several square stones placed several feet apart lead to the inner chamber. In the chamber stood a prominent iconic chair. At the ceremony, the leader would step on the square stones leading to the mystical chair. The priestess or Bobohizans began their rituals by chanting, calling the spirit to lead the chosen one to the chair. The moment he sat on the chair, he would be ascribed as the paramount leader of the Kadazan/Dusun tribe.

No other person was allowed to put their footstep over it. To step on it, would release the spiritual wrath of the guardian and caused suffering that might lead to death. After paying our reverence, we left the spiritual iconic building.

We continued our journey to Sandakan. On arrival, we checked into a hotel near to the memorial site.

We were free in the afternoon, so we contacted our uncle Joe Mariano whom we had not seen for ages. We wanted to pay homage to our ancestor who had died in Sandakan. Our uncle agreed to accompany us to the graveyard and show us the location. My grandma was born in 1898 and died in the year 1932 and my great great grandma was born in 1865 and died in 1926.

My grandmother buried in Sandakan Catholic Cemetery (1896-1932)

The resting place of my great great grandmother Vasinta Selvador Delgado in Sandakan Catholic Cemetery (1865-1928)

Ricky and I were pleased that we had fulfilled our quest to offer our prayer and reverence to both our ancestors at the Roman Catholic graveyard in Sandakan.

In the evening, we attended a dinner gathering at the municipal council president residence together with the Australian visitors who came purposely to attend the next morning event.

Hundreds of guests from Australia and local dignitaries were in attendance.

The reception dinner at the Municipal President's Residence in 2013.

The next day we were up early to attend the war memorial function. The event was accompanied by the sound of the bugle played by several Australian soldiers breaking the silence off the morning air. Finally, after placing the wreath by dignitaries, I was invited by the master of ceremony to the podium to recite the poem written by Bill Young.

Yesterday is not dead and gone; it's just resting

Yesterday, Today and Tomorrow. Partitions in time; following each other in sequence, they represent the past, the present, and the future.

In this trinity of Time, only yesterday is complete. Today is a blank sheet, while tomorrow, at best, is but a possibility.

Yesterday holds within it the timesheets of the past, the keys for today, and the hopes for tomorrow; which makes it the front runner in this, our trinity of Time.

Yesterday is the only roadmap we have, that has the streets marked in it, and that shows where we have been. At the very least, it can help in plotting life's journey; that is, if we have kept yesterday's map handy.

In life's journey, those who have kept in touch with yesterdays timesheets, will find they have, the where with alls, to make the most out of their trip.

Yesterday is where we have been.
Today is caught up in between
Tomorrow depends on where we have been.

Keep a close eye on yesterday's roadmap, and you won't get lost ....
Enjoy the trip.

by Bill Young

A beautiful poem written by Bill Young that I read during the event

The author Bryan Paul reciting the poem in 2013 written by Bill Young a POW in Sandakan in 1942-1945

Bill Young

A shape shot with a well-known writer Lynette Ramsay Silver who wrote the book BLOOD BROTHERS. From left: Ricky Azcona, Lynette Ramsay Silver and Bryan Paul Lai (Author)

Local guest at the function

The Australian representative and guest at the ceremony

The event ended at around ten in the morning. After breakfast, we drove to Kampong Gulam to see our old kampong. This was the village where we spent our childhood. All the kampong houses by the seaside were gone. The area where the fishermen had put their fishing net to dry was no longer there.

Instead, new hotels and the permanent building had taken its place. We left our birthplace at Kampung

Gulam in silence as we drove back to town. The only thing that stood by the side of the road near the hill was an old depleted building that was once used by my grandfather as his temporary gateway. We drove back and reached Kota Kinabalu in the evening.

The house where my grandfather used as his gateway in Kampong Gulam 1953

EPISODE 21

Penampang senior citizen (SCCB)

After the hectic assignment successfully concluded, I began to spend my casual time at the Sabah Government Pensioner Association.

During the duration of the Exco meeting, Fred Morris introduced another accredited senior citizen group which might be of interest to me. The activities currently being held at the Sabah Credit Cooperation Building in Penampang.

Joseph Jominol who was sitting beside welcomed me. He gave me the location of the building and said he would be waiting for me on that coming Wednesday.

The club was formerly mooted out by Tan Sri Simon Sipaun, the former Sabah state secretary.

Tan Sri Simon Sipaun

Moving On

His main intent was to provide the state pensioner with a venue for activities. Besides pensioners, other senior Penampang folks are also welcomed.

An avenue for the Penampang senior citizens to congregate once a week

An outdoor excursion by the Penampang Senior Citizen to Kokol Resort organized by the Sabah Credit Cooperation

Penampang senior citizen welcomed their interior counterpart

Activities are run on a weekly basis. Outdoor activities are organized once a year. Physical health activities and talks are part of the weekly event. In addition to the event, the Penampang Health Clinic provides a venue for a health check and other health concerned. These two organizations expose me to meet many seniors in Kota Kinabalu and Penampang.

Penampang Seniors having a good time at Kokol Haven Resort at Mengattal District.Inanam

Moving On

Penampang senior citizen reminiscing the old train ride from Kota Kinabalu to the interior of Sabah

EPISODE 22

Local underground resistance documentary film

In the year 2012 Doreen from Australia paid another visit to Sabah. She came with a professional cameraman Mr. Patrick. Her main aim was to make a documentary film, depicting the heroic deeds of the local people.

One of her associates Mr. Anub Singh had arranged to provide the vehicle, but it needed a driver.

I contacted my cousin Ricky if he could be of service. He agreed and I was thankful for his consent.

Incidentally, both Anub and Ricky's father were sentenced to death by the Japanese military court in Kuching.

Moving On

Doreen Hurst's arrival in Kota Kinabalu from left: Mr. Patrick the cameraman, Adrian Majaham and Doreen Hurst

Doreen and Patrick the cameraman arrived in Kota Kinabalu on 10 July 2012.

Adrian and I went to meet them at the Kota Kinabalu International airport.

In the evening, we had dinner at the Dovish restaurant at Jalan Bundusan. Several guests were invited such as Datuk Wilfred Lingham, former permanent secretary to local government, Datuk Kamal Quadra, former director of education, Datuk Thomas M and the welfare committee.

Dinner at Dovish restaurant sponsored by Doreen. In the picture from left: Datuk Thomas, Fred Morris, Datuk Kamal Quadra (Former Director of Education) and Datuk Wilfred Lingham.

I welcomed the guest and gave a brief preview of Doreen visit. I then invited Doreen Hurst to address the floor.

She spoke the reason why she was here, and her quest to make a documentary film about the war. She presented her version of her findings and factual events of the sacrifice made by the local.

After the speech, I thanked Doreen for her effort and the delicious dinner she had sponsored. It was a gesture of goodwill to express her very thanks to the Welfare Fund Committee.

Doreen Hurst addressing the guest during the dinner at Dovish restaurant in Kota Kinabalu Sabah

The next day, 11 July 2012 the documentary filming of those involved was conducted in my residence at Taman BDC Kelombong.

There were five of us involved in the short documentary film. Datin Theresa Regis started the ball rolling, followed by Mr. Anub Singh, Datuk Kamal Quadra, Ricatee Azcona and finally me. The session ended at around 3.00 pm.

From left Lilian Koh my wife, Doreen Hurst and Datin Regis at the author's residence

The next day 12 of July we travelled to Kundasang situated in Ranau Hamlet. We had two vehicles. One drove by Joseph Jominol and the other drove by Ricatee. We stayed for the night in Perkasa Hotel.

The next day we travelled to Paginatan 45 kilometers from Ranau.

A small kampong mainly inhabited by the Kadazan/Dusun and Murut tribe. Doreen's objective was to find the little girl who assisted the Australian during the war in 1941-1945.

We were lucky to meet her. She was sitting on the balcony with some relatives. After a short introduction and the usual greeting, we took our seat. We introduced ourselves and explained the reason for our visit. Doreen then spoke for a while, trying to reignite her memories during the time of her encounter with the escape allied prisoners.

In a soft calm voice, she apologized for not being able to rekindle her memories clearly. She was not well due to her recent ill-health. Doreen sat and waited patiently trying to listen to what she was trying to say. After a while, Doreen decided to let her rest, as she was not healthy enough to continue the conversation.

Meeting the little girl who helped the prisoner of war at Paginatan 45 kilometers from Ranau

From left: Doreen Hurst, the villager and Joseph Jominol my travelling companion

After a short discussion, we went back to Perkasa hotel at Kundasang, Ranau.

We met Anub Singh and his gang who came with his pals for a short holiday. We had a quick high tea at the restaurant before taking the day off.

Tea break at Perkasa Hotel Kundasang

The author Bryan with Anub Singh's compatriots at Perkasa Hotel Kundasang Ranau

Mr. Anup Singh, Patrick from Australia and Ricky at the table happy hours at Perkasa Hotel Kundasang

Moment of reflection, as Doreen touched the death March memorable stone in Ranau.

The next morning, we went to the third site situated at Datuk Dr. Othman property.

Datuk Dr. Othman's driver met us at the site and escorted us to their Homestay which was about 2 kilometers away. We met Datuk Dr.

Lungkiam who welcomed us and served us with fried banana, Tenom coffee and Sabah tea.

Just a chat with Datuk Dr. Lungkiam at his homestay

Datuk Dr. Lungkiam homestay in Ranau

After the visit, Joseph Jominol and I returned to Kota Kinabalu. Doreen, Patrick and Ricky continued their journey to Beluran and Sandakan. At Beluran, Doreen was fortunate to meet Datuk Kangkawang bin OKK Keluang.

After the video session and dinner, they stayed for a night before proceeding to Sandakan.

They met Gabriel Funk and Alban Lagan in Sandakan. They visited the Anzac Memorial Park and other relevant sites.

On 17 July Morning, Patrick flew from Sandakan to KK international airport. I met him at the airport and had some video session taken before leaving for Australia.

Visit to Roma little goat project

Doreen and Ricatee returned to Kota Kinabalu the next day after finalizing all the required schedules. Doreen accepted my invitation to stay at my house. The next day I brought her to see the goat farm at Fred's house compound sponsored by a kind lady Roma Little from Australia.

The hut built by Fred Morris to keep the goats donated by Roma Little. Doreen watching the animal feeding time

Doreen at Roma little goat pen. Fred Morris standing behind

Doreen left on 20 July 2012 back to Australia.

She conveyed her thanks to all those involved, especially to Mr. Anub Singh who provided the use of his vehicle for nearly ten days. Ricatee for driving Doreen around from Kota Kinabalu to Kundasang, Beluran and direct to Sandakan and all those who had helped her in her project.

EPISODE 23

Reaching out to relatives and old pals

Our recent trip with Doreen had finally come to a closure, as she made her way back to Australia. We were happy to have given her all the help she needed.

After taking a break for several days, we began our plan to reach out to old friends and associates of the past.

We believe that friends are important. We need to get in touch with them. We do not have much time as we are living in our golden years. Friends come and go but good friends are hard to come by. Cherish what you have and it will be a long way to make your life interesting and full of fun.

After a long search, several of our old friends began to appear.

Friends such as, Lawrence Wong Sau Fah, Datuk Clement Jaikul, Heron Paul Berry, Annie Hee, Irene Maluda, Jose Sikayun, Fanny Sikayun, Richard Primus, Douglas Primus, Datuk Douglas Lind, Maureen Lind, Jeffrey Rajaya and Ernesto. All these friends are either my buddies during the good old days of school or had lived in Wallace Bay, Sebatik Island when we were still little boys and girls.

Group of my friends who were with me during the launching of my first book "The Joy of Life" From left: Rose Chin Josie Sikayun, Jenny Azcona, Annie Hee, Adrian Majaham, Norma, Bryan the author and Datuk Dr. Florentious Epin Banaik

Ricky (sitting down) on his birthday gathering with the rest of the relatives at Inanam old town Kolombong as a token of our appreciation for his good work in helping Doreen Hurst in her film project

From left: Adrian Majaham, Bryan the author and Lawrence Wong Sau Fah. At the back-Mrs. Lawrence Wong

We met Lawrence Wong at the Luyang clinic dispensing medication to patients. He was surprised to see us. He has retired, but his service was still needed by the ministry of health. He was pleased to meet us, but could not spend much time due to his duties. Nevertheless, he promised to contact us as soon as possible. A month later we met again at a coffee shop.

Lawrence was originally from Semporna. A small coastal town that has an abundance of sea products.

Semporna was known to be an unsafe town. A town that was sporadically attacked by pirates in the past. In one incident, Albert Watson, the district officer, was having dinner with his family when the sound of gunfire broke the silence of the night.

He knew the small contingent of police on duty could not repel the intruders. He had no other choice but to take his family and ran into the nearby jungle. It was a close call. Several of the shops were robbed and an old woman died from her wound.

As promised by Lawrence, we met at a well-known coffee shop in town. A week later several other old pals met at an open restaurant at Jalan Bundusan.

We had with us: Jeffrey Rajaya, Ernesto, Adrian Dominic and Lawrence Wong. The casual got together brought us back in time. We had so much to talk about, especially my very old pal Jeffrey Rajaya whom I knew him since 1950.

Jeffrey's father and my father were both working in Lahad Datu. There were no schools in the district, so both of us were sent to Tawau. I was sent to the boarding house in 1950. Rev Father Crowder the visiting priest to Lahad Datu brought me in. That was the first time I laid my footprint in the school.

During that time, there were only three depleted old houses. I could still remember the time when we had no place to study. We had no other choice but to walk one kilometer away to a small building in Belunu road that belonged to Mr. Anthony Chan for our studies.

For our drinking water and other needs, the Tawau River was our only supply. We used kerosene lamp for our studies.

The Holy Trinity Boarding house in 1950. Those I could remember were: Top first Joseph Celaya (Kim Tong), Joseph Ho Ten Lok, Jeoffrey Rajaya, John Chin, Joseph Pairin Kitingan, Aming and Vun Hock Chung.

In 1941, the school was occupied by the Japanese Military as their garrison.

The compound close to the river was used to detain prisoners. My former boarding mate Joseph Ho had lots of stories he could recollect. Detainees were interrogated and tortured by the riverside. As a result of this, the school compound was known to possess some ghostly figures. In the middle of the night, we could hear screams and noises resembling human in agony. When the war ended in 1945, all the buildings were destroyed by the allied bombers. It was the boys and the priest in the boarding house that rebuilt the school through their hard work.

When Rev Father Bekama came in 1956, he started to raise fund and build more classrooms. He built the St Clare's Convent and several nuns were posted to the convent. The boarding house for outstation students was upgraded. Bunks were built and camp beds were no longer in use. The wooden church was replaced by a concrete church. In 1960 the secondary school had just begun. In 1962 two blocks of the secondary school were completed and we were asked to carry our own desk and chair to move to the new building. The present Holy Trinity was fully utilized by the primary school.

I have personally witnessed the transformation of the school from 1950 to 1963.

The development of these schools could not have made if Rev Father Bekama was not posted to be the rector of the church and schools. He built the St Clare convent to accommodate female students from outstation. Many girls living in faraway villages were able to continue their studies.

When Rev Father Sham came, he bought several pieces of land adjacent to the church compound. In 1965 the St Ursula convent was built through the effort of Rev Mother John Bosco and the Holy Trinity Parish Council. Another milestone to accommodate the education requirement in the Tawau district.

With the help of Gabriela Remedia Lobos, Mrs. Hong Teck Guan, Mrs. Albert Watson, the Malaysia Military and others, the St Ursula Convent was finally completed. A joint effort by the Tawau Catholic community

Our get together drinking session lasted the whole evening and left the restaurant at around eleven o'clock. The next day Mr. and Mrs. Lawrence invited me and my wife for a short trip to a Taiwanese coastal restaurant at Putatan for lunch

A wonderful reunion launch at the Taiwan restaurant on the way to Papar from left: Lilian Koh, Bryan, a Taiwanese lady (Restaurant proprietor), Lawrence Wong and his wife

We had a wonderful taste of crunchy roasted pork leg which was one of its specialties. Lawrence was able to locate several old boarding mates. One that crossed my mind was Mr. Andrew Thien who had a keen interest in black magic and charm.

Bryan Paul Lai the author and Andrew Thien in Tawau, 1961

Finally, Lawrence managed to trace his whereabouts. Lawrence took me and droved on. I was surprised when Lawrence brought me to the hospital. He was in the hospital bed lying with tubes all around him due to his ailment. I felt so sad to meet him in such a condition. I tried to call his name but could not get any response. He might have suffered dementia as he could not recognize me. Feeling sad and disappointed, I held his hand praying for his early recovery and left.

Several months later I was told he had gone to the Lord and entered the realm of the spiritual world.

Another friend that I longed to meet was Paul Jaikul, the younger brother of Datuk Clement Jaikul, was my best friend in the boarding house.

I met him twenty years ago in Tawau when Datuk Clement was the district police commissioner of Tawau. Paul was with him as Datuk Clement was trying to find a cure for him. He had some neurology defect when he hit his head on the house pillar whilst playing with his friends.

Since then his mental capacity to think properly had reduced. I did not make any effort to locate him. Then in the year 2016, I was told he had just died and regretted that I did not meet him earlier.

Another person that I used to know was Mr. Orlando Harumal. His parents' house was just across the road of Holy Trinity School. The last time I saw him was at the annual general meeting of the Sabah government pensioner association in Maksak building ten years ago. He could not recognize me although we were related through the marriage of my younger brother Daniel to his niece.

Adrian and I joined the senior citizen group and the historical society. We became life members, but our interest was short lived.

Adrian then joined the Sabah Government Pensioner Association as a life member. He was active for a while and held the post of Assistant Secretary, but later left and concentrated more on the Alpha group in the church.

As the days continued to pass, there were many old encounters that came on our way. We met Heron Paul Berry and Brother Pascal.

Heron Paul Berry and Wong Sau Fah

The following month Annie Hee rang me up inviting Adrian and me to a gathering at the Runway Café at Tanjung Aru hamlet.

The reunion had been successful as old memories came to the fore. Adrian and I sat there trying to compete with their chattering. The Ladies could not stop prattling as they hugged and reminisced old stories.

Reunion of seniors at Runway café Tanjung Aru, Kota Kinabalu

Annie the leader of the group broke the ice and welcomed all those present. She thanked Irene Maluda from Australia, Maureen Lind, Josie Sikayun, Rose Chin, Maureen Azcona, Jovita Azcona, Norlia Jalil, Biant Kaur, Velma Fernandez, Hasnah Harvey, Rose Majaham, Adrian Dominic and me.

As we were about to leave Annie proposed the last drink for the road and promised that another reunion would be held with more participants.

Meeting buddies of yesteryear. These friends were originally studying at Holy Trinity School. Tawau

Moving On

That offing by Annie on our first reunion came several months later when more ex-Students of Holy Trinity School were able to meet at the Cruise Café.

Besides the normal pals that came during the runway café, several more old distinguished ex-students of HTS were added to the list, such as Mary Lu, Geoffrey Tann, James Ku, Robert Lau, Fred Labunda, Datuk Clement Jaikul, Paul Berry, Lawrence Wong, Rose Majaham, Ben Fung, John Majaham, John Lee, Teo Leng Kiang, Michael Lutam, Henry Khoo, Fanny Sikayun, Peter Raymond Wong and wife, Regina Liew, Datuk Wahab Sulaiman, Elizabeth Wong, Rose Chin and Joseph Lee. This was the last reunion of 2017 that Annie managed to galvanize.

The next unofficial reunion of this group might be held in Tawau in the year 2018. A reunion which the golden seniors will be looking forward to.

Boys and girls of Ex-Holy Trinity School Tawau reunion at the cruise

Old boys at the Café Kota Kinabalu. Datuk Douglas Lind chatting with Jeffrey Tan

Birthday celebration with my second cousin family in Kota Kinabalu 2017

Moving On

Old pals at the reunion event at Cruse Café Kota Kinabalu

The old pal from Tawau Datuk Douglas Lind and Datuk Sahara Ismail

Meeting the old friend from Tawau on her birthday Puan Christina Liew, my former chairlady of St Patrick Primary School building fund

A surprise visit: Lilian's brother and sister in law Jenny from Tawau

Buddies since 1957: From left Mr. Paul Ku, self and James Ku

On my recent visit back to my old hometown Tawau, several friends met together.

From Left Thomas Voo, Justin M. and our jolly Francis Lin at his Japanese restaurant

Datuk Ramlie, Bryan the author and Haji Arastam

Old students previously studying in SMK Kuhara met at the Tawau airport after 35 years. From left: Datuk Haj. Ramlee Marhaban, Bryan Paul Lai the author and Haji Arastam Haj bin Pandorog from Semporna

Moving On

Cora Primus of Penampang who left for Australia years ago returning to visit Sabah and bring back memories of Tawau from an old friend from Wallace Bay

Connie Lupang sweet memories at Holy Trinity School Tawau, as she returned from Australia to visit old long lost pals in Kota Kinabalu. Connie at far right

EPISODE 24

The pulse of the nation

A good wellbeing nation lies in the core value of the family. A Greek philosopher once said that the third force or the citizen force in any community knows the responsibility and respect on the right of their neighbors. A society that lives up to the name of friendship and friendliness. Those who care and concern of their neighbors and are not impaired by selfishness and self- interest. This is a civil society that we are all longing for. But such values have to start from the family cell. So, it is imperative that we need to foster closer ties to the family and to the community at large. "Adab" is the highest level of a civilized and educated citizenry. What we do to others will have an uncanny way of hitting us from behind in many ways. Worse, such insightful actions may have serious repercussions on others who may turn this new Malaysia into the old Malaysia. Spoken by Mr. Tajuddin Rasdi a professor of Islamic Studies at UCSI University

Reaching out to my extended families in Sabah is part of my pursuit. Many of the older generations had gone, and the links become narrower by the day. The few bridges that still exist are mostly out of the country. My uncle Paul Lai Kui Siong is the only linkage from the last generation. He had migrated to Australia but came back to celebrate his birthday in Kota Kinabalu.

Then in the year 2018, a new link cropped up. My cousin Andrew Lai in Australia was able to make some contacts with lost family clan throughout the world. It would be another element for me to complete my family clan, which I started many years ago.

Uncle Paul Lai Kui Siong birthday held in Kota Kinabalu

Besides, Uncle Paul yearly pilgrimage, I do have some relatives that currently putting me in touch with the rest. My first cousin Ricky Azcona, my second cousin Margaret Kwan and the family of Aunty Theresa Tung (My father's sister), my uncle Patrick Lai, Andrew Lai from Perth Australia and Datuk Godfrey Lim, have played an important part to update me the necessary data on the family clan.

A wedding reception brought the family together
at Sacred Heart Cathedral Kota Kinabalu

Throughout my stay in Kota Kinabalu. I have attended several events such as marriage, birthday parties and funeral services. As a result, I was able to meet and to know them better.

Family get together at Taman BDC Kelombong

To meet before the sunset from left: The author Bryan, Aunty Rose Fung, Gabriela Lobos and Uncle Peter Chia

The Lai Fatt's clan (My grand Uncle's Family)

Granduncle Lai Fatt's Clan

EPISODE 25

A peek look at the Sabah Government Pensioner Association

The pensioners in the state from both the state and the federal government have increased significantly. In 1998, the retirees felt that an association to look into the needs and welfare of pensioners were overdue. The objective of PPKS is to galvanize and promote awareness amongst pensioners. The Registrar of societies approved their application on 29 December 1998.

At the vanguard of these initiatives were the former Sabah State Secretary Tan Sri Simon Sipaun, Mr. Terence Liau, Mr. Stephen Chin, Mr. Lee Ming Tet and Mr. Ho Wing You. In the year 1999, a Pro-Term committee was formed.

The Sabah Government Pensioner Association Committee in 1999

The followings were duly nominated to oversee the smooth running of the body: Mr. Terence Liau (President) Mr. Philip Liew (Vice President) Mr. Stephen Chin (Secretary) Mr. Dennis Lim (Asst. Secretary) Mr. Philip Ng (Treasurer) Mr. Liew Kim Fatt (Asst. Treasurer) Alan Koh, David Woo, Peter Koh, and Chin Kim Pin (Members)

The early pioneers of PPKS at the installation and fellowship dinner

Moving On

The executive committee of the Sabah Pensioner Association visited several major towns in Sabah. After visiting Sandakan, they moved on to Tawau in July 1999. They had their gathering at the Tawau Municipal conference room.

Several pensioners were present at the brief meeting. The president Mr. Terrance Liau then proposed an interim committee be formed to look into the association's interest. The following members who were present were nominated.

Group photo showing members of the Tawau Area Committee taken in 1999.

Sitting L-R: *Mr. Jagendar Singh (Secretary), Tuan Hj Fauzi Kau Yee Ching (Chairman), Mr. Steven Tandahan (Vice Chairman), Mr. Thomas Voo (Treasurer)*

Standing: *Mr. Ho Lee Ngiew (Member), Mr. Justine Gabriel (Member), Madam Catherine Tan (Member), Mr. Edward Supi (Member), Mr. William Kong (Member)*

The first Tawau district coordinating committee

Mr. Fauzi Kau served on the post for several months and resigned due to poor health. Mr. Jagendar Singh then took over as the new chairman. He was assisted by Mr. Stephen Tandahan as the vice chairman, Mr. Christopher Chong as the secretary, Mr. Thomas Voo as the treasurer and four committee members, Justine, Saiki Munta, Benedict Gakim and Ho Lee Ngiew.

My encounter with the association

I have retired for two years since 1998 but have not heard of the association until I was at the Tawau recreation club. I met Mr. Christopher Chong the secretary. After mentioning to me about the association, I submitted my form and approved by a membership No of 1234. (a lucky Number, I presumed.) In the year 2003, I received a notice of meeting at the Tawau Recreation Club. This was my first attendance, and I went early to take my place at the conference room.

Mr. Jagendar Singh the present chairman took the chair and welcomed all present. The secretary and the treasurer's report were tabled and passed as there were very few matters to discuss. Finally, as the other matters were concluded Mr. Jagendar Singh announced his attention to step down and resigned with immediate effect.

The members were surprised, as there was no indication that he wanted to call it a day. Mr. Jagendar Singh proposed Mr. Stephen Tandahan the vice chairman to take over. Mr. Stephen was not present but had sent words he would not accept due to health concerned. The committee requested Mr. Jagendar to reconsider his resignation. Mr. Singh was adamant and refused to retract his resignation.. No one wanted to take the hot seat. Finally, all eyes were on me and urged me to take up the post.

As a novice, I respectfully refused, but after unanimous backing from those in attendance, I unenthusiastically took the job. The meeting ended at around noon time.

On my way home, my mind was on a roller coaster, thinking of the situation I was put in. The two-former chairmen had difficulty to mobilize the pensioners to join the association. I would be facing the same predicament unless some financial support in the offing.

The first committee meeting that I had was at my residence. The meeting was casual and friendly. We discussed matters pertaining to the coming general meeting. The venue and date were proposed and passed. The meeting was held at the City Club opposite the Marco Polo Hotel. At the gathering, lunch was provided, sponsored by a close friend and associate of mine Mr. James Ku Hien Leong. All the incumbent retained their post.

The committee met once a month, to review matters of interest pertaining to the current development of PPKS in Sabah. As the district chairman, I attended several meetings in Kota Kinabalu. This quarterly executive meeting enabled me to meet other exco members of the association.

Tawau Area Committee (2003-2004)

Sitting L-R: Christopher Chong (Secretary), William Kong (Vice Chairman), Bryan Paul Lai (Chairman), Thomas Woo (Treasurer)
Standing: Ho Ngiew @ Ho Lee Ngiew (Member), Jagendar Singh (Member), Justine Gabriel (Member), Saiki Munta (Member)
Not in the picture: Steven Tandakal (Member), Yong Oi Teck (Member) and Benedict Gakim (Member)

The Tawau New Committee members

Friendly social visit by Pensioners from Kota Kinabalu..

Pensioners from Kota Kinabalu took a short social and study tour of Tawau. They came from the 20 to 23 September 2003. The Tawau committee, Justin Gabriel, Thomas Voo, William Kong, John Chang and I were at the Tawau Airport to welcome them. The group was led by Datuk Godfrey Lim and Datuk Richard Yapp.

Datuk Godfrey Lim and Bryan Paul Lai (Author).

The first destination in their itinerary was the Balung Resort. A well-known location owned by the former chief minister of Sabah, Datuk Harris Salleh. Mr. Arul, the field manager, welcomed them.

The Balung River Resort was first owned by Mr. John Anselmi. It was later sold to Datuk Harris the former Chief Minister of Sabah

Part of the view of the Balung Resort from the hill side

A unique river stone mosque built by the former owner Mr. John Anselmi. The stones were taken from the river nearby.

Datuk Harris joined the group at tea time and dinner. After dinner, Datuk Harris Salleh invited the visitors to his getaway corner for happy hours.

The next morning, after breakfast they assembled at the conference hall for a brief discussion. After that, they were brought around the estate to witness the various projects available in the estate.

In the afternoon, the visitors left for Tawau and checked at the Monaco hotel. The next day they visited the Teck Guan Cocoa Factory at Tanjung Batu.

On the way back, Datuk Godfrey Lim, Datuk Richard Yapp and I paid a courtesy call to the Tawau Municipal Council President Datuk Harieth Munjung.

In the evening, we had a fellowship dinner with Datuk Harieth as the guest of honor. The next day after lunch at the Japanese restaurant at Fazar complex, they flew back to Kota Kinabalu.

The guest thanked the Tawau committee for their warm reception. During their visit, I was able to inculcate friendly ties with Datuk Godfrey Lim and Mr. William Tham Peng Loi. Both of them were Deputy Presidents of the association.

I was pleased to be acquainted with them. My close link with them gave me the right channel to be involved with the association and its members. An opportunity to increase my friendship to all retirees in the states. However I need to thank Mr. William Tham Peng Loi, the deputy president of PPKS for putting me up during one of the annual general election. As a result of this proposal, I have served in the committee till this very day 2018 I defined this as the significant moment for me to enter into the pensioners' fraternity. It keeps me busy and enjoys every part of it.

From Left: Mr. Yee Thien Shon of Tuaran pensioner, Bryan Paul Lai and Mr. William Tham Peng Loi the deputy president of PPKS

Moving On

Being a member of the Sabah Government Pensioner Association, provided us the occasion to travel to every district to learn of their woes..

The executive committee of the Sabah Government Pensioner Association (2010-2012)

Keeping the body fit by having a good exercise. Promoted by the Minister Datuk Hajah Jainab, Datuk Sri Panglima Hai Ahmad Ayid

The association has gone through challenging times with leaps and bound.

The leadership has continued keeping the association relevant through times.

The first President Mr. Terrance Liau, a former associate of mine came from Tawau. After Mr. Liau retired, Dr. Epin took over and governed for ten years. In the year 2014, Dr. Epin wanted to take a break to concentrate on his business. Datuk Wilfred Lingham was nominated and won the presidency unopposed.

President of PPKS Datuk Wilfred Lingham

The new President, Datuk Wilfred Lingham had a daunting task ahead of him. With his experience and competence, many of us knew that he would be able to make a difference to the association. We are greatly confident of his leadership and ability and can move the association to greater heights. A series of brainstorming session was initiated to find ways and means to archive this aims.

His new Secretary-General, Mr. Hamit bin Harun was at the right place and time. With his vast experience in the government administration level, he had tons of ideas up on his sleeves.

Moving On

Encik Hamit bin Harun
Secretary General of PPKS

Mr. David Ho the treasurer of PPKS

Several programs were mooted out. It was difficult, but gradually the activities organized by the association came out positively.

As a result of this new approach, many retirees began to show some interest and came in droves to be members of the association. The time to lure the rest of the forty-five thousand retirees has begun

Part of the program introduced was to initiate twenty district coordinating committees throughout Sabah. A task which is formidable, but achievable. Through the effort of every district coordinating committee, membership has increased. Since Datuk Wilfred took over the association, the membership strength has increased to 4450 members from 2800 when the new group of elders took over..

Each district is given their autonomy to organize their activities. PPKS Kota Kinabalu will provide nominal financial help within the means of the association.

With so many districts to care for, the main committee needs to monitor their yearly activities. It has to provide some financial and moral support.

As a member of the committee, I have the opportunity to accompany the top executive on their monthly visit. An opportune time for me to dig old stories from pensioners that I met.

The Executive Committee of the Sabah Pensioner Association and 20 District Coordinating Committee from 2016-2019

Moving On

The AFO Subcommittee of the Sabah Government Pensioner Association 2018. Sitting down: from left, David Ho, Datuk Wilfred Lingham. Standing from left: Albert Oh Abai, Joseph Wong, Abdul Hamid Harun, Stella Wong, Hajah Hasnah Harvey, Evelyn Lim, Bryan Paul Lai, Quirine Angkangon and Joseph Jominol

The President of PPKS Datuk Wilfred Lingham meeting high powered officers from Putra Jaya to discuss pensioner's woes.

PPKS taking part in Majlis Bulan Kebajikan MPMS 2018

PPKS AFO Committee at Suria Mall during Bulan Kebajikan MPMS 2018

Moving On

Datuk Wilfred Lingham President of PPKS presenting a plaque to the Minister YB Stephen Wong

A brief discussion amongst the committee of PPKS and the board of IDS in Kota Kinabalu

The President of PPKS Datuk Wilfred Lingham presenting a plaque to Tan Sri Simon Sipaun the chairman of THE INSTITUTE FOR DEVELOPMENT STUDIES (IDS) SABAH

EPISODE 26

Pra-Pesara seminar

This seminar is organized by the Sabah Government Pensioners Association. Its part and parcels of the association to make available correlated information to pensioners to be.

During our visit to the districts, we found that past pensioners had difficulty to acclimatize themselves upon retiring. They were not getting enough information pertaining to government's facilities and other relevant matters. As such pensioners were in the dark over many issues. It was due to these snags, that the association felt that seminar as this would help retirees to be. None of these could have materialized without the staunch support from relevant government bodies such as JPANS. (Jabatan Perkhidmatan Awam Negeri Sabah), the association managed to fulfil the aspiration of the retirees. Encik Hamit Harun is given the thumbs up for making it happened.

With the green light on, PPKS took the initiative to organize the first seminar in Kota Kinabalu. It was successful and the relevant government authorities were pleased with the outcome. During these past few years, the association had organized in Kota Kinabalu, Sandakan, Keningau, Tawau and Lahad Datu

Experience prominent speakers and those in the know-how were invited to partake at the seminar. Participants were provided free meals for two days.

At the seminar, the President took the opportunity to brief the pensioners on the role of PPKS. As a result of this briefing, many were encouraged to join.

The organizing Committee of Pra- Pesaraan Seminar

Tan Sri Simon Sipaun sharing his experience and thoughts to pensioners to be.

Seminar Pra-Pesaraan held at Dewan Kebudayaan Kota Kinabalu 2014. The first catalyst that spurred the PPKS to greater heights..

Seminar Pra-Pesaraan di Kota Kinabalu 2017

Seminar Pra-Pesaraan di Sandakan

Seminar Pra-Pesaraan di Keningau

Seminar Pra-Pesaraan in Lahad Datu

Seminar Pra-Pesaraan in Tawau 2017

Seminar Pra Pesaraan in Lahad Datu 2018

Seminar Pra-Pesaraan in Keningau 2018

Reaching out to Pensioners throughout Sabah

Besides the above events, the association has also embarked on other programs in collaboration with the medical department and other NGOs. Such as hearing, eye, glucose and growing old gracefully.

The DCC Program in Tuaran

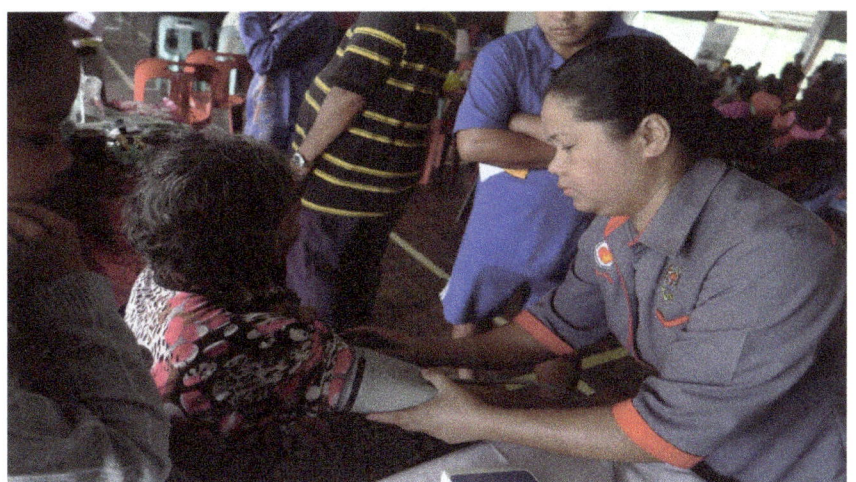

Checking blood pressure

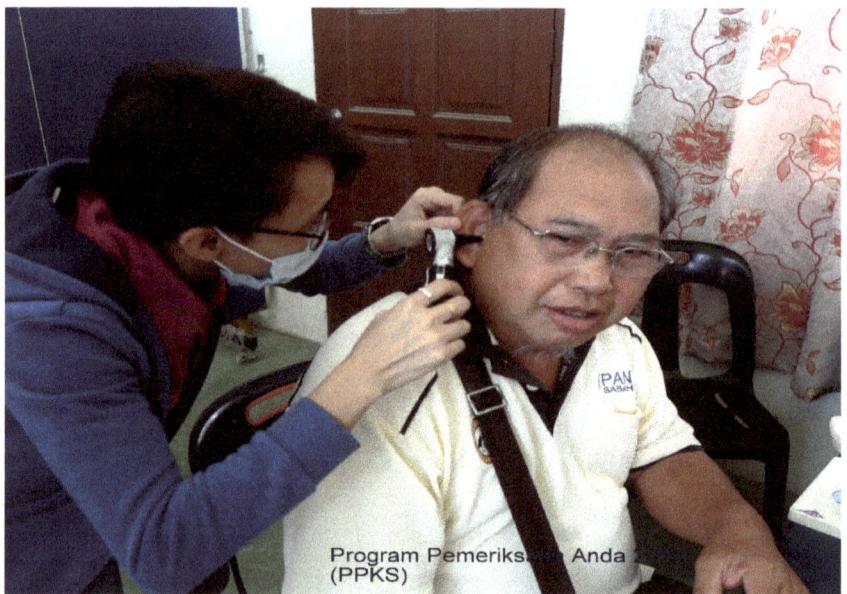
Hearing Program for seniors

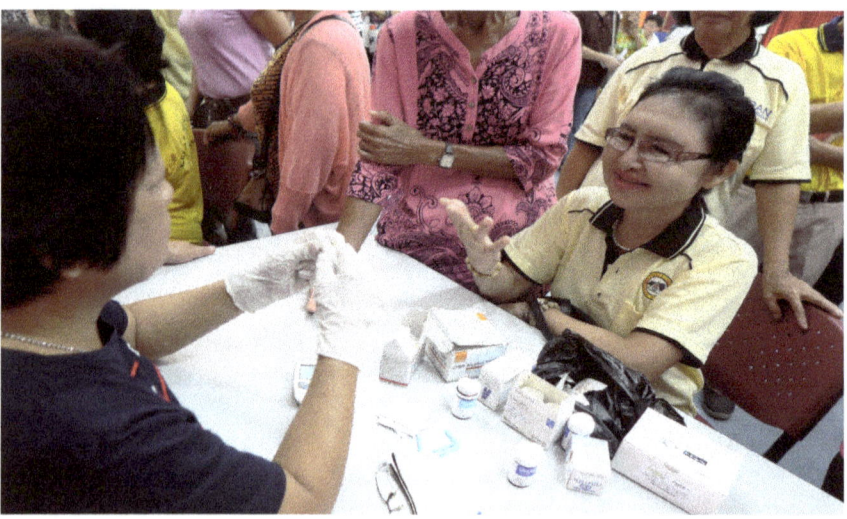
Checking blood Glucose in Penampang

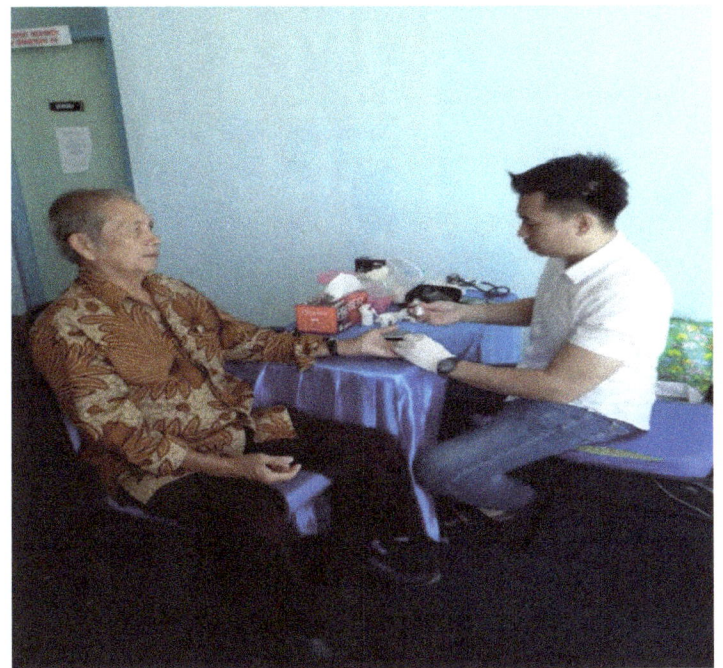
Health check in Kuala Penyu

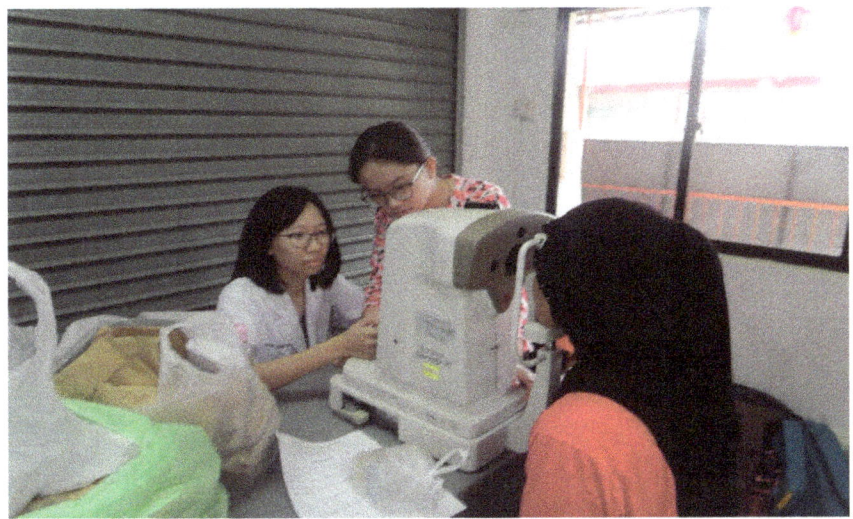
Eye testing program in Tuaran

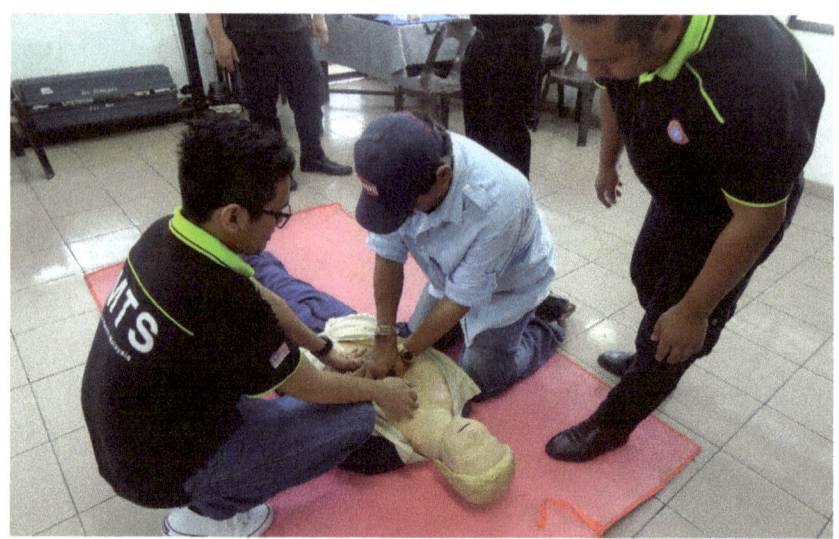

The President Datuk Wilfred learning to do CPR in Tuaran

The President Datuk Wilfred Lingham presenting a wheelchair to pensioner in Kuala Penyu

Moving On

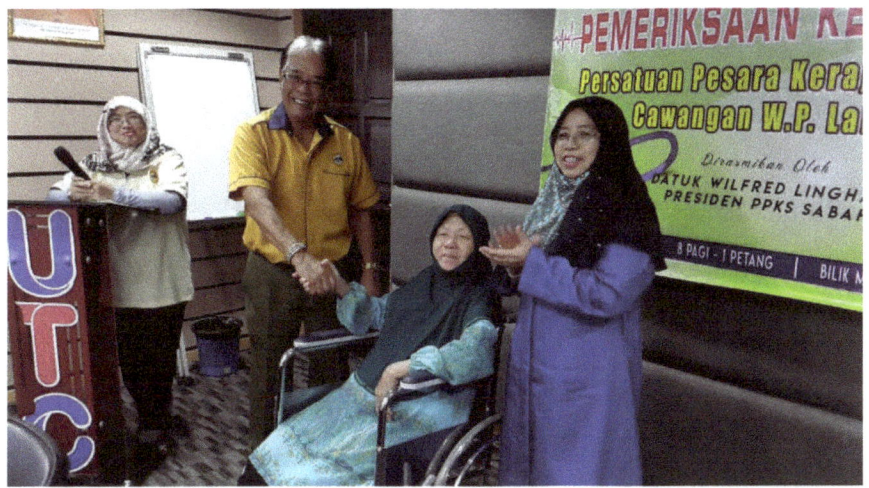

Handing out wheelchair to pensioner in Labuan by the president of PPKS Datuk Wilfred Lingham

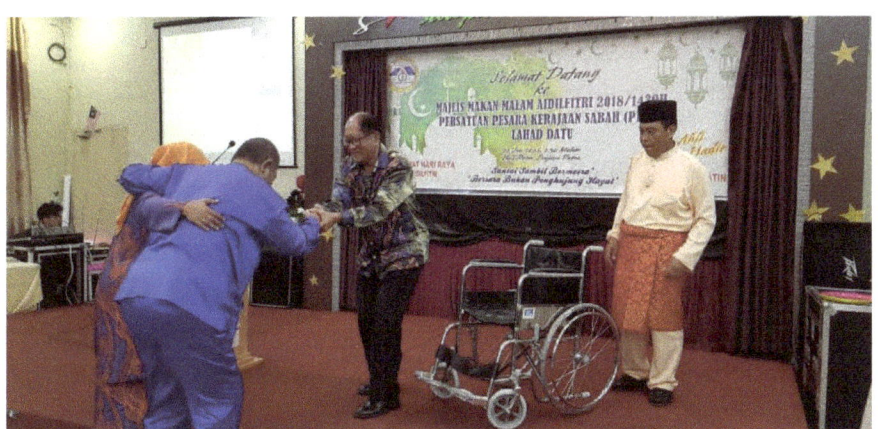

The deputy president Bryan Paul Lai presenting a wheelchair to a pensioner in Lahad Datu

The Penampang DCC chairman Joseph Jominol presenting a wheelchair to a member of PPKS in Penampang.

The MPMS, acronym for Majlis Perkhidmatan Majlis Sabah, has played a vital role to boost the activities of all NGOs in Sabah.

This organization is under the umbrella of the Hal Ehwal Penguna dan Jabatan Perkhidmatan Awam Sabah.

One of the highlights of their activities is the Social Month (Bulan Kebajikan) and the Appreciation Night (Malam Penghargaan) which are held annually. It is during this function that several awards are given to individuals in various categories such as TOKOH SUKARELAWAN KEBAJIKAN, ANUGERAH SUMBANGAN IKHLAS DAN SIJIL PENGHARGAAN.

PPKS President Datuk Wilfred Lingham receiving award Tokoh Sukarelawan Kebajikan from T.Y.T. Tun Datuk Seri Panglima (Dr) Haji Juhar bin Datuk Haji Mahiruddin Yang Di-Pertua Negeri Sabah in 2016

PPKS or Persatuan Pesara Karajan Sabah is an associate of the above organization. Throughout the years, several executive members of the association had been awarded. Datuk (Dr.) Florentious Epin Banaik, former president of PPKS and Mr Dennis Lim, former Secretary general of PPKS.. Recently in the year 2017, our renowned President Datuk Wilfred Lingham was awarded the Tokoh Sukarelawan Kebajikan.

Activities in picture depicting the various activities of PPKS

Courtesy call to the Sabah State Secretary by members of PPKS

Panel of speakers were invited to clarify the formation of Malaysia to pensioners in Sabah

From left: Datuk Wilfred Lingham Deputy President, Datuk Dr Epin the President, Mr Michael Ng committee member, Mr. William Tham Deputy President and Mr. Dennis Lim the former Secretary-General.

Members of PPKS attending talk on how to grow old gracefully in Penampang

Members of PPKS on outing mood at Tanjung Aru Kota Kinabalu

The PPKS think tank group discussing the future of PPKS in Lahad Datu

PPKS members on tour to Lahad Datu.

Closing ceremony of pra-pesaraan seminar in Tawau Sabah

The association has set up twenty district coordinating committees in most major town. Its main objective is to create an accredited body, a link to pensioners in that area. It would also enable the association to provide other necessary help.

Recently, the state government had allocated some financial aid. This helped to enable the association to provide laptop, printer, medical kits such as blood pressure and glucose monitor. Through the auspicious of other NGO, the association was able to provide wheelchairs to some of its members.

The PPKS AFO sub-committee has visited many of the district coordinating committee respective area. This was to provide moral support and recruitment of new members to the fold.

The DCC has played a constructive role to support and promote the welfare of its members within their rank.

The executive members of the PPKS visit Tawau to form the DCC and to pay a courtesy call to Tan Sri Liew Yun Fah From Left: Mr. John Chang, Bryan Paul Lai, William Tham, Datuk Wilfred Lingham, Tan Sri Liew Yun Fah, Datuk Dr. Epin, Wang Tsai Siah, Mr. Thomas Voo and Mr. Justin Majanggon

EPISODE 27

THE SABAH GOVERMENT PENSIONER ASSOCIATION DISTRICT COORDINATING COMMITTEE

A short depiction on the district of Sandakan (Little Hong Kong)

Sandakan town in the sixties

View of Sandakan in 1930. Courtesy of Datuk Wilfred Lingham

Old Sandakan Market 1950. Courtesy of Datuk Wilfred Lingham.

Sandakan is the second largest town in Sabah. During the British North Borneo Company, Sandakan was made the administrative center and a trading post after Kudat.

The word Sandakan derived from a Suluk words Sandakan which means "The place that was pawned", later it was named Elopura which means Beautiful town. It reverted back to Sandakan and become the capital of North Borneo in 1884.

The St Mary School in Sandakan

The St Michael Church and school in Sandakan

The St Mary and St Michael School had started very early during the early days. Many of the prominent leaders of North Borneo came from the said school. My father and uncles were sent to St Mary's school under Rev Father Parson during the colonial period. According to history the first Chinese appointed as the first Kapitan Cina was, Mr. Fung Ming Shan of Sandakan.

Sandakan is also my birthplace. I was born in Kampung Gulam close to the Batu Sapi area in 1943 during the Second World War. An area of mix indigenous tribe that built their houses by the shore.

My mother told me Sandakan was a peaceful place. People living harmoniously side by side for a generation.

During the Second World War, when the British army in Singapore surrendered, thousands of war prisoners were sent to Sandakan.

They were brought in by ship and interned close to the Sandakan present-day airfield.

During the pre-war period the "orang putih" as it was called (The White Men) was highly respected by the local inhabitants. The white man was addressed as "TUAN". The populace was utterly shocked to see them being brought in a humiliation manner. They were put in small huts packed like sardines. Basic amenities and proper food were minimum. Under such circumstances, many could not survive under such a grim situation. Medical drugs were brought in clandestinely by the underground to elevate their suffering. My father Peter Raymond Lai and his immediate superior Doctor Tylor were part of the team.

The clandestine operation was short-lived. They were betrayed by a member of the underground. The person responsible wanted to sell the medical drugs on the black market for personal gain. As a result of this treachery, members of the underground were arrested. They were incarcerated at the power station in Tanah Merah. Tortured, beaten then sent to Kuching prison to face the Japanese Tribunal court. Some were put to death and others remained in the Japanese prison as war prisoners. Those still alive were released after the Japanese surrender in 1945.

After the war, Sandakan was still under the Charted Company. Due to fiscal restraint, they relinquished their rights and administrative power to the British Empire. North Borneo was then made as the British Colony. Sandakan began to rebuild and the people once again were able to live in peace and prosperity.

Moving On

Hakka women in Sandakan helping to rebuild the town after the war. Courtesy of Datuk Wilfred Lingham

At the end of the war, raw materials were needed to rebuild many towns and cities caused by the war. North Borneo had much to offer and businessmen throughout the world came in search of building materials such as timber. Sandakan gradually became the economic centre of North Borneo and was once called "Little Hong Kong".

The Sandakan DCC.

From left: Philip Mosinoh (Chairman) Kinus Tuzan (Vice chairman) Norfaizah Abdullah (secretary) Eric Murut Keromok (treasurer) committee members: Matius Sodomon, Hamidah Hamzah and Betty Eddy

The Sandakan DCC chairman Mr Philip Mosinoh addressing the happy hours gathering

The Sabah Pensioners in Sandakan at one time was also under the auspicious of the Sabah Pensioners Association Kota Kinabalu. In fact, several of them were part of the pioneers that started the Pensioner Association Sabah. However, in the midst of their activities, some members proposed to break up from the main body and applied for their new pensioner's association to the Register of Society as a new entity. Having got the approval, the Sandakan pensioners formed their own association and split-up from the main body.

As a result of this split up, a new DCC was formed, headed by Mr. Philip Mosinoh. Mr. Philip was a former forestry officer and had ample connection to many pensioners. Under his leadership, Sandakan DCC had organized many activities. Our recent visit to Sandakan was the testimony of his proactive action. PPKS had organized pra-pesara seminar in Sandakan and the response was overwhelming. So far, the Sandakan DCC continues to make effort to recruit more members and to assist those that need help in the process of their coming retirement.

The short historical depiction on the District of Tawau

Tawau taken from the building of Lai A.Hotel 2013

Tawau town as seen in the year 2013

Tawau was first named as TAWAO and then renamed TAWAU. The only well-known industry in the past was in Kalabakan prefecture. It was known to be the biggest coal mine in the world. It supplied coal to many ongoing steamers around the world. When the coal mine stopped its operation in 1935, most of the inhabitants left and settled in Tawau.

There were many Japanese enterprises involved in plantation and the fishing industry. After the war, most of them were repatriated back to Japan. Tawau began to develop, shops and wooden houses were built everywhere especially along the seafront.

Tawau had also being occupied by the Japanese as mentioned earlier. As a result of the Japanese occupation, several mysteries had been passed along the populace on hidden wealth hoarded by the Japanese.

Hidden Loot of the Japanese.

During the Japanese occupation, many of the town folks had either lost their gold to the Japanese or the old folks buried their possession under the ground. After the war, the Japanese knew that they could not bring the stolen gold to Japan so they buried it in uncertain areas known only to them. In the year 1990, some village boys got some information from an old man on the location of hidden gold at BAL estate. Trying to keep it secret, the treasure seeker worked at night digging until they reached several meters in an underground cave. They could not go further as it was completely dark. To assist them to continue the search, a generator was used to support them in the dark. Unknown to them, the emission of the poisonous carbon dioxide gas caused their breathing difficulty and had to withdraw from the tunnel in a hurry. Some managed to escape but few could not make it and died on the spot. It was a tragedy of ignorance of the nature of the noxious gas that killed them. The hunt for treasure came to an end and the tunnel was sealed by the authorities.

Till to this very day, the supposedly hidden gold remained a mystery and its secret unresolved.

The Ming Dynasty Jade Mystery.

I like to highlight something of interest that spurred my curiosity. I was at a friend shop to meet the owner, and old friend. A small jade was lying on the table beside a small saucer. It was a small jade that embossed with some Chinese character. I was somewhat curious and wanted to know where the jade came from David, told me that he bought the jade from an old man staying at the foot of Tinagat hill. The piece of jade he found came from an old hidden cave up on the hill. Not knowing the importance of it, he sold it to David for a few Malaysian ringgit.

I took the jade on my hand and scrutinizes the object. On the surface stood some Chinese character clearly marked, I presumed it was from the Ming Dynasty era.

According to the old man, the jade was found in an underground tunnel by chance.

Only the old man who had lived there many years ago, knew the right location. He was reluctant to expose the exact place.

I was somewhat curious and wanted to find out the truth and the exact location the jade was discovered.

David told me the old man had a few more in his possession. The story intrigued me and was determined to look into the bottom of the mystery. We were staying not far from the hill. Every evening I looked at the top of the hill and contemplate whether I could climb. I knew it was not an easy climb. The area was completely covered by secondary jungle and wild undergrowth. To ascend up the mountain without a proper guide would be mission impossible. Months passed, and my hunt gradually died down and out of my intrusive mind.

During the phenomena of dry weather hit Sabah, many parts of the state were experiencing bushfire. Tawau did not escape the scourge. I was at the Tinagat beach setting up my net when suddenly I saw the fire up on the hill. It burnt for several days and spread the whole area from the top right up to the foot of the hill. A week later the fire was gone and the hill looked bare.

This gave me the opportunity to look into my mission once more. I wanted to find the mystery of the jade.

I decided to ask my brother Ambrose to accompany me to explore up the hill. As an adventurous person himself, he greed

Before the climb, we had everything ready and nicely pack for our oncoming trip. The weather was hot and some ember was still visible all around the vicinity. We managed to find our way up the peak, in spite of the steep climb. We combed the whole area, hoping to see a cave or underground hole. After searching for more than an hour without any success, we decided to call it a day.

Before descending, we sat for a while under a rock and took a glance of Tawau town and the view of Cowie Harbor. We were tired and disappointed, but still full of spirit.

The view of Tawau from our location was awesome and breathtaking. After taking some pictures we began our journey down the hill. We arrived at the base an hour later.

With an unwavering determination, I decided to make another shot at a later date. Before that, I needed to locate the old man and let him guide us up the hill. So, I went to Kampung Muhibbahraya to locate an old friend who knew the old man well. I decided to invite another good friend, who was currently the prison department head Mr. Vincent Raja.

Accompanied by my friend, we went to Tinagat to locate the old man. We went to his house but was told that he had moved out and went to stay in Balung. Unable to locate him we decided to finally put an end to our dream. We had missed the scope of the century. A revelation that could put Tawau in the map, to discover the historical episode in the history of Sabah.

Tawau District Coordinating Committee

The DCC Tawau provides a health check to pensioners and the senior citizen at the Tawau Central Market

DCC Tawau providing community service at the Tawau Sin On Market

The Tawau DCC has been in existence since 1999. In the past, the committee has not been active due to financial constraint. After I left Tawau, Mr. John Chang took over. John later relinquished the post due to health reason and was taken over by Mr. Ho Lee Ngiew. With the full cooperation of the central committee in Kota Kinabalu, the DCC began to imitative several activities. As a result of their various activities and positive action, many retirees joined as members. The central committee in Kota Kinabalu provides them all the assistance both financially and moral support.

A get-together after the pra-seminar organized by PPKS and in collaboration with the Tawau DCC.

Sitting from left: Mr. Thomas Voo, Mr. James Ku, Tan Sri Simon Sipaun, Datuk Wilfred Lingham, Mr. Bryan Paul Lai, Madam Evelyn Lim and Mr. David Ho Siew Hien Standing from Left: Mr. Ho Lee Ngiau, Mr. Justin, Lucy Leong, Encik Hamite Harun and several DCC members

Moving On

A short historical depiction on Kudat district (Tomborungan town)

Kudat town in 2016

Kudat is situated in the coastal area. A town teeming rich with products from the sea. Kudat is also known as the tip of Borneo, close to the territorial water of the Philippines. Kudat could be a tourist haven for international travelers if the security situation improves

Kudat was formerly known as TOMBORUNGAN by the Rungus tribe. During the British North Borneo Company, officers of the company had some difficulties in the pronunciation spoken by the Rungus people. As a result of this misunderstood word between the two parties, the officers inadvertently pointing to the well-known grass called Kutad. The Rungus tribe thought that the English officer was referring to the grass called Kutad. As a result, of this interpretation, the officer called the town Kudat, replacing the original name of Tomborungan.

Tamu in Kudat in 1908. Courtesy of Datuk Wilfred Lingham

In the year 1880, the British brought in many Hakka's from Hong Kong to work in the industry, especially in the coconut plantation.

In the year 1881, the British North Borneo Company discovered oil not far from Kudat town. They made Kudat as the administrative centre.

Many expatriate officers of the British Company were stationed in Kudat, on the presumption that the discovery of oil could bring the bonanza for the company. Their dream was shattered, as the oil fields they found were not economically feasible during that period.

In the sixties, Kudat was just a small town and the only town that known to have a three-headed coconut tree.

My last visit to Kudat town was in the eighties with a good friend Mr. Johnny Chong, a local lad from Kudat who wanted to pay a visit to his farm in the hamlet. He continued his studies at Gaya College as a trained teacher. After graduation from college, he was assigned to a school in Tawau call SRK Andrassy. In 1971 he was transferred to SMK Kuhara. Johnny invited me to accompany him to Kudat to visit his land.

We drove all the way from Tawau and rested in Kota Kinabalu. The next day we drove to Kudat.

Before returning to Kota Kinabalu, we bought some Kudat famous ground peanuts, coconut candy and Hakka favorite food called "CHUN KEN".

Moving On

Pensioners visit Kudat DCC

It's more than thirty years since my last visit. I was looking forward once more to see this once famous town at the tip of Borneo. The Kudat Golf Club was the first golf course built in Sabah, built in 1900. The only golf course in North Borneo, formally affiliated with the St Andrew golf club in Scotland.

I visited Kudat with members of the Sabah Pensioner Association in 2015. We stayed in a hotel next to the Chinese Temple. I was walking along the streets when I saw a prominent sign named Jalan Chin Sham Choi.

I was told by one of the men sitting in the coffee shop that it was the name of a very prominent person who lived in Kudat in the early days. He could not provide me with any more details as I tried to learn more. As I walked further, I noticed another name was written on another street called Jalan Wan Siak. I presume that these gentlemen might have been someone of high standing in the Kudat community. However, the reason why their names had been immortalized came to light, when I met Mr. Patrick Chin at a dinner in Sutra Harbor Banquet Hall. We were both sitting at the same table and after our normal friendly conversation inadvertently came to know that Patrick's granddad was a resident of Kudat. As I enquired further, I was surprised to learn that the street name which I saw was named after his grandfather and the other named after his great-grandfather on his mother's side. It was indeed coincident to meet him, and an opportunity to dig further into the historical facts of his family legacy. I was then told that his grandfather was born in St Francisco in 1879. At 8 years old his family moved to Hong Kong. Subsequently, the family moved to North Borneo in the 19 centuries. Patrick's grandfather sent his son Chin Sham Choi to Hong Kong to continue his education. After graduation, he returned to Kudat. He was well versed in both English and Mandarin language. Due to his proficiency in both languages, he was able to help many of the poor folks of Kudat, especially in dealing with the British Authorities. He was so generous to the underprivileged folks that they called him a good philanthropist. Occasionally he was asked to help to settle some land dispute and acted as an unofficial lawyer with no charge. He travelled to many towns such as Sandakan and Jesselton to help folks that needed his service. He started the Chinese Chamber of Commerce in Kudat and subsequently provided his service to start the

Jesselton Chinese Chamber of Commerce. As an enterprising entrepreneur, he was able to send his children to China for further studies. Whilst as son Chin Chi Vui (Patrick's father) was sent to Singapore then to Sandakan. Chin Sham Choi died in 1942 due to illness.

Mr. Chin Sam Choi of Kudat town 1879-1942 Courtesy of Mr. Patrick Chin

As to the other street called Jalan Wan Siak, it was named after Patrick Chin's great-grandfather on mother side. He came from a well to do family in Southern China. Due to his close encounter with the authorities, he was forced to flee the province and migrate to North Borneo in 1924. He was financially strong and was able to own several properties in Kudat such as shop houses and coconut plantation. He employed many workers and had contributed much to the community of Kudat, hence as a token of the community's gratitude to him, they named the street as Jalan Wan Siak.

My recent trip to Kudat in 2018 has given me another positive perception that Kudat hamlet will have a big potential of becoming a tourist hub in the very near future.

The tip of Borneo in Kudat hamlet, Sabah Malaysia

The tip of Borneo, Kudat Sabah Malaysia

The tip of Borneo has made drastic changes since my last visit twenty years ago. Several new motels and hotels were built at the seafront. With more motel, hotel and high-end hotels, Kudat could one day be the best tourist attraction, Sabah has to offer. One that attracts the most is the Kudat Rivera Private Beach Villas, an exclusive place for the high-end tourists.

The attraction to divert city life at the tip of Borneo in Kudat.

Kudat Riviera Private Beach Villas at Kudat hamlet Sabah

Moving On

The Kudat Riviera Beach Resort

The Kudat DCC

Sitting from left: Michael Muniandy (Secretary), Evan Wong (Chairman), Liew Kong Yin (Treasurer), standing from left: Philip Lee, Tai Moi Yuk and Liew Tze Kong (Committee members)

Q and A with Kudat pensioners

The Government Pensioner AFO Committee had put Kudat under its radar, and had visited several times to provide moral support. The Kudat hamlet is large and many pensioners are living in scattered villages. This is one of the factors that DCC Kudat could not increase the intake of retirees. The chairman Mr. Evan Wong has promised to look into the matter and hopefully with the new committees recently nominated would find better days ahead..

Kudat DCC at their general meeting

Moving On

A short historical depiction on the Ranau district (Mount Kinabalu)

Mount Kinabalu lies in Kundasang, Ranau Sabah.
The highest mountain in South East Asia

The Ranau Hamlet

The name Ranau came from the Dusun word Ranahon which means paddy field. Over a period of time, the word Ranahon was shortened to Ranau.

The Ranau hamlet has been one of the most well-known and exciting districts in Sabah.

Kundasang, a suburb of Ranau, stands at the highest mountain in South East Asia. The most awesome sight and beautiful scene that captures the mind and soul of Sabahan. Undoubtedly, it might be the height of the Kinabalu Mountain that acts as a bastion to fend off the fury of the usual typhoon that happens in the Sulu Sea. The Kundasang area has been declared by the international body UNESCO as the World Heritage Site.

Kundasang is the place where every Sabahan should make a visit to enjoy the wholesome beauty. In the past years when I was still in the service, Kundasang was the only place that I had never missed bringing my family for a holiday.

The main attraction that entices visitors to visit, is the mighty mountain itself. Besides the cool mountain air, the verities of flowers, temperate vegetables such as cauliflowers, cabbages, spinach, the cattle farming and the tea plantation.

The gateway to the tip of Mount Kinabalu

On the way to the foot of the mountain lies the world-famous international golf course situated at the base of Mount Kinabalu.

The Kundasang Golf Course

The Kundasang War memorial. Kundasang, Sabah, Malaysia

The War Memorial and the biggest Dairy farm in Sabah are right in the epic centre of the Kundasang town. Further down to Ranau town on the way to Sandakan, is the Poring Hot Spring and several interesting areas for visitors to indulge in.

Ranau tea plantation resort

Further away from Ranau, a former legacy of the Mamut copper mine. A mine operated by the Japanese company but had long abandoned. Now it stands a big lake of untreated toxic substance which could be an environmental disaster if it enters into the main river streams.

Ranau DCC

PPKS President Datuk Wilfred having the discussion with Ranau DCC.

Ranau district coordinating committee

The comprehensive health clinic organized by Ranau DCC

The Exco committee of the Sabah Pensioner Association Kota Kinabalu has designated Ranau to be an active DCC. It is led by Mr. Aloysius Labi as the chairman.

In the year 2017, some Sarawak pensioners visited Sabah. They came here for a week tour of the State.

Pensioners from Sarawak visiting Sabah. 2016

The Ranau DCC was given the duty to organize a welcome fellowship event. They did a good job and the visitors were impressed by the cooperation and warm welcome by the pensioners.

Their study tour of Sabah had been a memorable one and in reciprocate invited the Sabah Pensioners to visit Sarawak.

Moving On

A short historical depiction on Papar town (The flat Land)

The old building of Papar town

The opening of Papar Bridge in the early years of North Borneo. Courtesy of Datuk Wilfred Lingham

The name Papar came from a Bruneian word means flat land. Papar was once ruled by the Sultan of Brunei. The first known leader of Papar was Datuk Amir Bahar. Later handed to Overbeck and Dent brothers in the year 1877.

My Lai family clan that first migrated from China settled in Papar. My father was born in Papar and my great-grandmother had a farm at Kampung Manis. My father who was just a young kid at that time used to piggyback on grandma's basket as she walked to the tamu ground to sell her farm product.

Papar was occupied by the Japanese during the war. When they surrendered in 1945, Allied soldiers were sent from Labuan to accept the surrender seal from the Japanese in charge of the town. The allied soldiers passed through the village of Datuk Dr Florentious Epin Banaik. Florentious was just a little boy. He was excited as the contingent of smart looking Australian soldiers passing at his village. The children were given sweets and other goodies. The Japanese were all rounded up and enclosed at the Papar field with barbed wires before being dispatched back to Japan. Many of the locals were having their great days as they witnessed the Japanese soldiers being put in an enclosure. Before the war ended, the Japanese were behaving like kings expecting everyone to respect and to bow as they passed. Now the locals had the last laughs as they saw they deranged Japanese being sent away in trucks to Jesselton for repatriation back to Japan.

In spite of my generation was from Papar, I had never visited the town until 1965 when I got the opportunity to attend a youth seminar organized by the Sabah Association of Youth Club.

TYT Pengiran Ahmad Raffae Pengiran Omar

Datuk Donald Stephen

YB Thomas Jayasuria

The then Chief Minister of Sabah, Datuk Donald Stephen and the TYT Pengiran Ahmad Raffae Pengiran Omar were both in attendance to officiate the event. Thomas Jayasuria was also present to address the youth leaders attending the function. Our first youth President was Mr. Yapp Pak Leong. The second time I visited Papar was in the year 1968 with a group of scouters; Gaya College Scout Troop. We hiked all the way from

Kota Kinabalu by following at the side of the Railway track. We camped at the Buang Sayang beach for two nights and three days.

Previously the only route to Papar was either through the Limbahau narrow road or by train. With the new road completed the drive took only forty-five minutes.

Papar District Coordinating Committee

Sitting from left to right, Benjamin Dantol, (Secretary)Mohd Farid Mohamad Amin (chairman) Antin Joseph (Vice chairman), Ruslan Menggil (Treasurer) Standing left to right Rupin Gunting,Puam Rusa Kuntiong,Puan LengAh Len@Doreen,Puan Flora DavidEncik Abdul Hamid bin Majah and Elias Jouni

Hearing aid program in Papar DCC

The chairman Haji Mohd. Farid Amin addressing the members

Papar DCC general meeting held in the year 2018

Previously, the membership recruitment in Papar was slow.

Spurred by the president Datuk Wilfred Lingham, the Papar DCC surprisingly succeeded to increase their membership by several fold.. As a result of their hard work, Papar DCC managed to win the membership drive competition and won a sum of RM 1000 in 2016. The present chairman is Haji Mohd Farid Haji Amin.

Moving On

A short historical depiction of Beaufort town (Japanese garrison)

Beaufort town in the olden days

Beaufort is a small town, the gateway linking the capital of Kota Kinabalu to Sarawak border at Sindumin. The town was named after Leicester Paul Beaufort, the British Governor of North Borneo. Before Beaufort was chosen to be the settlement, there was three small village existed in the vicinity: Kampung Kalaban, Kampung Mesilau and Kampung Malulugus.

The Charted Company settled the natives in the interior, the Chinese traders and other ethnic groups in town. Most of the inhabitants are from the ethnic tribe of Muruts and Bisayas. Beaufort is ideal for the planting of rubber trees. As a result of the rubber boom in the early 1900 facilitated Beaufort to a huge economic boom, but now most farmers opt to plant oil palm instead.

During the Second World War, Beaufort was occupied by the Japanese. The Japanese high command made Beaufort their strategic command centre. At the onset of the end of the Second World War and before the signing of surrender by the Japanese commander, a fierce battle erupted between the forces of the Australian and the Japanese.

An allied soldier by the name of Leslie Thomas Starcevich who fought bravery to take over the town was awarded the Victoria Cross.

On 17 September 1945, a separate instrument surrounded was signed by general Akasi. Beaufort was chosen as the meeting point to assemble and to repatriate to Japan all the staff from headquarters, the soldiers and civilians of the Japanese from the west coast and the other district.

Children going back to school after the war in 1946.
Courtesy of Datuk Wilfred Lingham

I have visited the town numerous times, in the hope of locating the site of my grandmother's graveyard. She was buried in Lingkungan catholic cemetery. In spite of my search, I could not find the exact spot.

Beaufort District Coordinating Committee

The Beaufort DCC with the executive committee of PPKS

The Sabah Government Pensioner Association had visited the area several times. The main aim was to provide moral support and some financial assistance. Our recent visit to the year 2018 has shown some improvement. The DCC needs extra exertion to attract retirees in the district to join the association. The present chairman is Mr. George Groroi.

A short historical depiction on Tenom district (Fort Birch)

The town Tenom was formally known as Fort Birch. A strong bastion of the Murut tribe and made as their unofficial capital. At the centre of the town stood the stature of Ontoros Antonom (1885-1915). In 1915 Ontoros led the Muruts against the British Charted Company in the Rundum village of Tenom. This event was known as the Rundum Revolt.

A statue of the Rundum Revolt in Tenom

Tenom is well-known for its fertile soil. The agricultural department has played an important part to provide high-quality fruit trees to the farmers.

I have not made any visit to the town in the last twenty-two years after the war. It was only in 1967 that I tried to locate my uncle which I had not seen since 1956.

I took a train from Tanjung Aru to Tenom. My uncle Joseph Lai was surprised to see me and invited me to stay at his house.

During my second visit in the year 2015 with members of the Sabah Government Association, I noticed that Tenom has improved greatly and many new shop lots and concrete buildings have dotted the landscape.

The strong team of PPKS from Kota Kinabalu
visiting Tenom to show their support

The chairman of the District Coordinating Committee Mr. Yacob Mushal Khan welcomed us and invited us to have a simple dinner at his residence.

At the hotel, I was able to have some casual conversation with Datuk Wilfred as we were drinking on our cool beer.

Datuk Wilfred Lingham now residing in Kota Kinabalu

Datuk Wilfred spoke of his younger days in Tenom. Trying to maintain his poser, he began to describe the inhuman behavior of the

Japanese. How he had witness of hand and in a person of what his father had gone through.

During the Japanese occupation, government officers especially the expatriate was summarily rounded up and detained. Normally they would be interned as Prisoners of war and sent to Kuching prison camp in Sarawak.

To make the matter easier for the Japanese, they brutalized and tortured them to such an extent that they died from the thrashing with no accountability.

One such government officer who suffered the most was Mr. Patrick Lingham, Wilfred's father. He was working at the telegraph office which was the main communication nerve centre to send and receive messages beyond the shores of North Borneo.

The Japanese zoomed on his duties and considered to be detrimental to the Japanese security. The high command decided to take immediate action to curb this threat.

Mr. Patrick Lingham was unaware of the danger about to befall his family. He was at home resting from a day's hard work at the office. He was just about to have dinner with his family when the dogs in the compound yard were barking continuously. Thinking that some neighbors were making an unscheduled visit, Mrs. Patrick Lingham went to open the door. Right in front of her eyes were several Japanese soldiers armed to the teeth. Her face turned pale and was in fright as she called her husband.

The Japanese burst in, showing their audacious behavior and void of any courteousness. They immediately took Patrick Lingham by the arm and dragged him out of the door.

Mr. Patrick Lingham tried to reason with them, but was ignored and roughly pinned him down to the ground. He was kicked several times in his abdomen. Mrs. Lingham cried and begged for mercy and tried to pull him up as blood oozed out from his mouth.

Patrick stumbled the second time, as Mrs. Lingham tried to raise him up again. Wilfred, Patrick's young son watched with horror as he witnessed the incident right in front of his eyes. He had never in his innocent mind to contemplate such dreadful and wicked people ever existed in this world. Little Wilfred who was only several years old, was clinging to his mother crying loudly and tried to reason in his innocent mind the reason why the Japanese threat his father like a dog.

What had his father done to deserve such cold-hearted battering? That undesirable incident fully embedded in his innocent mind until this very day.

Mr. Patrick Lingham was then taken out and brought to some bushes out in the field to be roughened up. They continued to beat him up until blood oozed out from his mouth the second time. He laid motionless with no sign of bodily movement. The Japanese satisfied that they had given him a good thrashing left, with one last kick on his head. Hidden among the bushes were several of the Murut tribe observing the whole episode at a distance

The Murut tribe hiding among the bushes

They felt so sorry for him but could not intervene. They were armed with blowpipes and arrows. It could not match the Japanese rifle, as they watched with repugnance.

As soon as the Japanese left the scene, they carried him to their village deep in the jungle. They nursed him back to his health with herbs. Mr. Patrick kept hidden throughout until the war was over. After the war, Mr. Patrick Lingham came out much to the thrill of Mrs. Lingham and son Wilfred.

Mr. Patrick Lingham and some of the villages who had been tortured by the Japanese went to the detention centre. They gave the Japanese captives a good beating, under the very nose of the Australian soldiers who watched in glee.

The ordeal that the Langham's family suffered had a lasting memory to Wilfred for the rest of his life.

Mr. Patrick Lingham who was still not fully recovered from his suffering had to be nursed back by Mrs. Lingham. He resumed his duties at the telegraph office in Sandakan and Tawau before being sent to Jesselton as the director of Telekom department.

The Tenom DCC committee

The Tenom District Coordinating Committee

Membership drive and hearing program in Tenom

The following morning, we attended the scheduled meeting with members of the Tenom pensioners. As usual Datuk Wilfred Lingham gave his short speech and provided some advice and encouragement to the members.

The pensioners in Tenom was once an active body. Since then, it had lost its resourcefulness. Hopefully, our visit would kick-start a new beginning.

A short depiction on the historical aspect of Tuaran town (Sir Stanford Raffles),

Tuaran in the eyes of the laymen seemed no historical significance. However, it was interesting to note that Tuaran had been recognized as one of the settlements that Sir Stanford Raffles took interest in the year 1813. Sir Stanford Raffles was the governor of Java. He wanted to seek permission from his government to accept the invitation by the Sultan of Brunei to curb the piracy problem that was rampaged at Jawaran in the north of Borneo. Jawaran was the name of a Malay word Tawaran. It had two meanings. The first means fresh water, implying of its importance to the local community. The second means "to bargain" which referred to the economic activities of the people in the tamu ground which had been going on prior to the British colonization in the year 1884.

The Dusun Lotuk people of Tuaran produce a traditional liquor called Bahar made from coconut sap mixed with a kind of tree bark. The other most well-known iconic food famous in Tuaran is the "Tuaran mee" or "Dua Ah Lan Men" made by the Hakka people.

The first time I visited that hamlet was in 1965, paying a courtesy call to my uncle Mr. Paul Lai Kui Siong. He was attached to the district office as a district officer. During my visit, he took me around Tuaran to see the imported Bali cow which Tuaran was known for. In those early days of the charted company era, there was no road linking Jesselton. The only way to travel down to Jesselton was the concrete underwater bridge passable only during the dry season. Otherwise, they had to travel by bamboo raft.

The bamboo raft was used during flood season linking Tuaran and Kota Kinabalu

Travelling to Tuaran, we need to pass several towns such as Inanam, Mengattal and Talipok. Upon reaching Tuaran on the right side on the way to Ranau stood a small town called Tamparuri.

Previously the Tuaran pensioners had to submit their application to the PPKS Kota Kinabalu. It was only recently in 2016 that the President Datuk Lingham proposed to have the DCC in Tuaran so that pensioners in the township could look after their own affairs.

Moving On

Another location of interest in Tuaran is the Tuaran Mini Ants Museum located on the road to Kota Belud

Members of PPKS at the ant museum

The author at the giant replica of the ant

The Tuaran DCC

The committee members of Tuaran DCC

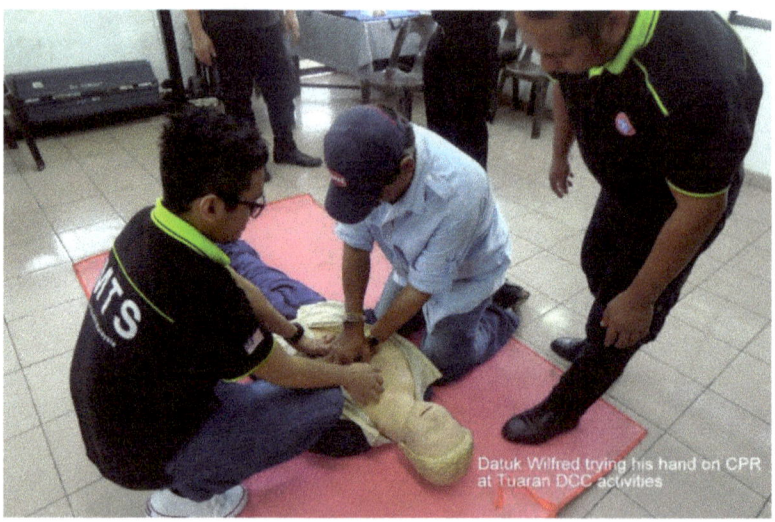

The Tuaran DCC health clinic. President PPKS Datuk Wilfred Lingham learning the art of CPR

The Health Clinic organized by Tuaran District Coordinating Committee

The present chairman duly elected is held by Mr. Michael Goh. With him holding the helm, the Tuaran DCC has organized many activities. Furthermore, the membership participation has increased.

Our moral support in Tuaran has boosted the district coordinating committee. As a result, more activities will be in the offing.

A short historical depiction of Keningau town (Koningae town)

Keningau town

Keningau town in the year 2018

Keningau is the fifth largest town in Sabah. The name Keningau derived from an abundant of Javanese Cinnamon tree known as koningae or Kayu Manis in Malay.

The iconic stone in Keningau (Batu sumpah)

The most iconic Oath Stone was erected by Sargent Major Garukoi Giurun. It was officially unveiled on 31 August 1964 when Malaysia was finally formed. It depicted a strong conviction by the people of Sabah that the rights enshrined in the constitution must be upheld at all cost. The town rose up on its peak during the economic days of timber boom. Now the oil palm plantation has brought in to replace the timber era.

Australian Engineers constructing the Keningau Sepulut road in 1964-1966 Courtesy of Datuk Wilfred Lingham

Keningau had been a strong unit of PPKS. Now, the intake of members has been slow.

Keningau DCC actively participate in the Sook program

The Keningau District Coordinating Committee of PPKS

PPKS Kota Kinabalu is finding ways and means to recuperate the association slow intake. Many retirees in the district had not responded well, in spite of having the seminar and other activities in Sook prefecture. The present DCC chairman is Mr. Chin Chee Vui.

A short depiction on the Tambunan district (Kg Tibabar)

Tambunan Prewar

Tamu in Tambunan in 1930 Courtesy of Datuk Wilfred Lingham

Tamu in Tambunan in 2018 (Pisompuruan Square)

Tambunan is known to be the stronghold of the Kadazan/Dusun tribe. A district with undulating landscape and beautiful mountain ranges. A sleepy town with mundane economic activity. The economic lifeline is mostly paddy land and agricultural products. Tambunan is famous for its local wine called Lihing.

Mat Salleh and his men escaped to Tambunan after he revolted against the British and burnt the first British settlement at Gaya Island. With his men, he escaped to Tambunan. The British was high on his heels and finally caught him at Kampong Tibabar. Mat Saleh and his men fought the British in a gun battle on 1st February 1900 and was shot. The local tribe of Tambunan built a memorial for his bravery to go against the British Company.

Tambunan District Coordinating Committee

The Sabah Government Pensioner Association had made several visits to the town to revive the activities of the association. The DCC was subsequently formed, spearheaded by Mr. Patrick Juimn Paunil who became the temporary chairman.

Formation of the Tambunan DCC

Tambunan DCC at work

Meet the seniors and hearing program at Tambunan DCC

A short depiction on the historical aspect of Kota Belud district (James Brooke Range)

Kota Belud during the Charted Company 1930

Kota Belud is a midway town from Kota Kinabalu to Kudat. The town is considered to be the unofficial capital and gateway of the Bajau community.

Kota in the Bajau language means "Fort" and Belud means "hill" which means fort on a hill. Several hundred years ago before civil society became the norm and the introduction of a government administration, the various tribes often clashed amongst themselves. As a result of this antagonism, they often fought each other. Some tribes needed to find shelter to protect themselves from the marauding enemies. They had no other choice but to find a safe place as a bastion. The local Bajau tribe finally found the surrounding hills as their best site to protest themselves from their adversaries. As a result, the location they took was then known as Kota Belud.

Kota Belud is mainly populated by Bajau, Illanum and a trickle of the Chinese community. Besides the prominent mosque and Christian churches, there was also a wide-open space called James Brooke Range. On my several visits with the committee of the pensioners, I noted some progress in the development of the town in comparison to my last visit thirty years ago. Cattle farming and padi planting are the main economic activities.

The Kota Belud DCC

2015

Social event at Kota Belud DCC 2018

The deputy President Bryan Paul Lai representing the President Datuk Wilfred Lingham at the function.

The present chairman of the Kota Belud District coordinating committee is held by Awang Daud bin Awang Gati. With his leadership, the DCC Kota Belud has shown that they can move forward to make the district committee active and relevant. The PPKS Kota Kinabalu will continue to provide some financial and moral support.

A short depiction on the historical aspect of Semporna town (Tong Talun)

Semporna a seafaring town situated on the east coast of Sabah was formerly known as "Tong Talun" in the Bajau dialect. It means hujung hutan in Malay. Panglima Uddang Panglima Sallehangni and Panglima Saktig of Bajau Kubang ancestry were responsible for the name. The name gradually evolved to Semporna which means a peaceful and complete place. The hamlet was ruled by the Sultanate of Sulu before being handed to the British North Borneo Charted company in the year 1876.

In the past, government officers were apprehensive being posted to that town due to its insecure environment. Pirates used to attack the town as far back as in 1900. In 1950 the incursion by the pirates flared up again. Mr. Albert Watson was the District Officer and the man in charge of the hospital was Mr. Jaikul. The police lightly armed were no match with the intruders as the town came under attack. Mr. Albert Watson and several of the government officers took their family and hid in the jungle nearby until the coast was clear and the intruders had taken what they came for. During his term of duties in Semporna, Mr. Watson also discovered a hidden tunnel built by the Japanese beside the old police station. It was formally used by the Japanese to hide their weapons and soldiers during the air raid by the allied forces.

The steamboat or ship was the only mode of transport available. Reinforcement to protect the town had been difficult. After the incident, the authorities built a lookout tower and increased the strength of the police force with some lethal weapons on their hands.

The first time that I went there on board the Kimanis ship with my friend Lee Fah Sing and Martin Ho, was in 1965 to form the Semporna Youth Club. While the ship was still on the sea close to the wharf, hordes of Bajau kids as young as six years and above on their little canoes came close to the ship on all sides putting their little hands up, asking for tips, drinks or coins. It was a wonder that none had lost their lives through this dangerous feat

The Skull Hill in Semporna

The indigenous tribe of Semporna was mostly Bajaus, Suluk and undocumented seafaring people called the Pelahu. In 1969 after my graduation as a teacher, I was posted to this little town and assigned to teach at Semporna secondary school. I was here for a year and I had a pleasing time visiting many of the islands and kampongs. Most of my students were kind and very hospitable.

Neolithic period skull found in Semporna

There were some historical sites which had not been fully explored. There was a hill called skull hill. It was known to have been used by the Japanese to hoard their unlawful treasure. Some locals were put to death and dumped into the same pit. The Sabah Museum found several old artefacts that traced its origin from the Neolithic period as well as some Ming dynasty porcelain. The Sabah Museum had been on the site and continued to make its finding.

The Semporna DCC 2017

The Semporna DCC Committee Members.2018

There were many pensioners in Semporna but none as yet stood above the rest to lead the pensioners' interest. Datuk Wilfred Lingham has long subscribed that every pensioner in the state should be reached out and to be given the opportunity to take part in the Pensioner Association. He then took the initiative to pay a visit to the district to see for himself the response of the pensioners living in that area. The first meeting held at Tuan Haji Munduru house was promising. A temporary DCC was formed with his nominating committee. Tuan Haji Munduru Haji Mohd Noor became the first chairman. Hopefully, with his enthusiasm and interest, the district coordinating committee of Semporna would do well.

On 6 January 2018, a team of the executive committee attended the first event hosted by Tuan Haji Munduru with the cooperation of the DCC Tawau Lahad Datu and Kunak. The event was attended by many local leaders in spite of a slight shower during the event.

The chairman of DCC Semporna Tuan Haji Munduru welcoming the guest 2018

The District Officer of Semporna officiated the opening, Two books were presented by the President Datuk Wilfred Lingham of PPKS to the District Officer

The event was attended by PPKS committee from
Kota Kinabalu, Tawau, Lahad Datu and Kunak

DCC Semporna general meeting held on 6 September 2018

A short depiction on the historical aspect of Lahad Datu district (Neolithic)

Lahad Datu in 1928

Historically Lahad Datu had a long antiquity. It dated back to the 15 centuries, one of the earliest inhabitants of North Borneo. Several excavations were made and unearth many Ming dynasty Chinese Ceramics. The Idahan and orang Sungai might have come from the part of the Asian continent thousands of years ago of Austronesian migrants to Sahul during the Neolithic period.

Several studies were made by the Sabah Museum to unearth the historical aspect of the find. They needed to make further excavation to trace back the people who dominated at Darvel Bay thousands of years ago. Further to the east is the village of Tungku. A well-known pirate lair in the past. It was the base for pirates in the last century. Based on the manuscript found in the Idahan language dated 1408 AD., Islam was first introduced in the region. The man who might be responsible was an Idahan by the name of Abdullah who embraced Islam in Darvel Bay.

In the eighties, my chum Johnny Chong and I had to travel to Lahad Datu to invigilate several secondary schools for the public examination. We had to travel to Tungku at Felda Sahabat. We had been assigned by the Ministry of Education to oversee and to supervise the public examination at the district. The main economic activity was timber and as timber began to deplete, the planting oil palm has started on a large scale. Lahad Datu did not escape the scourge of piracy. Couple of years ago, the bank in Lahad Datu was robbed by armed men dress in military uniform. Several bank staff were killed.

The Tandua incident

The Philippines claimed to Sabah which has not been resolved indefinitely once again manifested into an ill-fated incident.

A self-proclaim group of intruders from the Philippines managed to infiltrate into the shore of Tandua in Lahad Datu.

Two hundred and thirty-five armed militants arrived at the shore of Tandau Village on 11 Feb 2013. They called themselves "The Royal Security Force of the Sultanate of Sulu and North Borneo". This group was sent by Jamalui Kiram 111.

The Malaysia military forces surrounded them where the group had assembled. The military negotiated with them to leave the country, but they refused. Finally, the military had no choice but to take stern action. At the end of the standoff about fifty-six militants, six civilians and ten security personals were killed. The rest of the militants escaped and some were captured. The standoff lasted till the 24 March 2013.

Lahad Datu DCC

The Lahad Datu District Coordinating Committee of PPKS

Presenting wheel chair to pensioner in Lahad Datu

Malam Mesra in Lahad Datu DCC

The district coordinating committee of the pensioner association was formed in the year 2015 lead by Haji Dardi bin Shawal, the present chairman. Since then on, pensioners have begun to show interest in the movement. Haji Dardi bin Haji Shawal has provided an alternative channel to pensioners to indulge in extra conduit for healthy activities.

A short depiction on the historical aspect of Kunak district (Madai)

The entrance to Kunak town

Kunak, a small plantation town located close to the coastline. I*ts* main economic lifeline started with the timber industry. With the declining of the timber era, large areas of the hamlet have transformed into oil palm plantation. In the sixties when most of the jungle was still intake, the area was teeming with wild animals. During the second world war of 1941, the Japanese military had set up a garrison in Kunak. There were several abandoned Japanese graveyards left unkempt.

The ethnic tribes consisted of mainly Bajau, Bugis and with a sizable of Chinese community running most of the Kunak shops. A Cocos and Kadazan settlement scheme are located few kilometers away near to Giram estate. Along the Giram estate road, we found some historical site that had been cordoned by the Sabah Museum. Few pieces of old artefact were discovered but had not been fully unearthed by the authorities to trace its origin. Besides that, several caves were also found in Kunak. The most famous one is called the Madai Caves, a natural bird sanctuary. The Idahan from Lahad Datu walked for weeks to harvest the famous bird's nest. During the Second World War, the Japanese had also built a long tunnel to protect their weapons and other war materials, from the constant bombardment of the allied planes.

Kunak District Coordinating Committee

The Kunak DCC Committee 2018

In the beginning, PPKS had no plan to set up a district coordinating committee due to its limited number of pensioners in the district. However, due to the request by some pensioners in the hamlet, Datuk Wilfred Lingham, the PPKS president decided to give the pensioners in Kunak a chance to participate in the PPKS activities. The present chairman is Haji Renti Mukibban.

A short depiction on the historical aspect of Beluran district. (Buludan)

Beluran was first named as Buludan or Bundan. The first Englishman who went to the town a hundred years ago found the native words Buludan or Buudan which mean hills in the Tidung language, found it difficult to pronounce. Another word they used to call was Buad or Bulud. To make it short the European called it Beluran which till today remains as Beluran.

In spite of my birthplace in Sandakan or had stayed there from 1953 to 1954, I had never visited that area. Only faint memories of the word Beluran came to mind when several of my relatives worked in that hamlet. Beluran was also occupied by the Japanese during the Second World War.

Many Javanese laborers were brought in from Indonesia to work as porters during the dreaded death march of the allied prisoner of war. This was according to Datuk Haji Kangkawang who is still living in Beluran. Datuk Haji Kangkawang was just a young lad when the Japanese entered the village.

Moving On

During his early days, he studied at a Vernacular School in the year 1947, two years after the war. He continued his schooling in St Michael School Sandakan. He then went to Kent College and trained as a teacher. After his training, he taught in Jesselton, Sugut and Libaran. After teaching several years, he entered into politics under the USNO banner. In 1966, he got a Colombo Plan to study in New Zealand. At his retirement home in Beluran, he could still rekindle the days during the war of 1944.

His father Panglimah Kulam was the headman of the hamlet when the Japanese entered the village. He and his men were forced to build the huts for the Japanese. Food was scarce as most of the small shops were closed. Alongside the Japanese soldiers were hundreds of starvation prisoners of war, forcibly repatriated from Sandakan to Ranau on foot. The journey was tough as they had to walk through jungles, hills and crossing the deep ravine. Many died or left half dead on the way in the jungle. Kulim could not stand to watch the Australian soldiers being treated like animals and the humiliating situation they were in.

Without proper food, water and medical needs, many succumbed to their ordeal. Unaware by the Japanese soldiers, Kulam decided to make an escape plan. As the Japanese guards were not on full alert due to fatigue, Kulam could make the move. Kulam waited for the right moment as the bad weather was approaching. Suddenly there was an outburst of thunder and the rain came pouring in. The Japanese were all running for cover. Kulim and several soldiers then made a dash into the jungle and disappeared for good. Knowing the terrain well, he could easily evade the Japanese. The group went into a secluded village where Kulim and the prisoners could recuperate. When the Japanese realized that Kulim was missing, they searched for him high and low. The Japanese were then told by the Javanese porters that Kulam had been eaten by the crocodile.

After the war, Kulam aided the Australian military to trace out the route and to collect all those who had died and brought them to Labuan for proper burial. Kulam was appointed as the native of the state and awarded Panglima as the paramount leader of the native tribe.

Till today, there is an old myth that the Japanese had buried some gold treasure in Beluran, but still could not be traced. The populace that made Beluran their home could be summarized as follows: Tidung, Orang Sungai, Kadazan/ Dusun, Suluk, Chinese, and several others.

The Beluran DCC

Through the effort of Mr. Philip Morsino, the chairman of Sandakan district coordinating committee, the Beluran DCC was formed in 2017.

Mr. Longinus Kim Tuan became the first chairman of the district committee.

The Beluran District Coordinating Committee

The first general meeting held to elect the temporary DCC

A short depiction on the historical aspect of Kota Marudu district (Bandau)

Kota Marudu was formerly known as Kota Bandau. In 1974 it was changed to the present name of Kota Marudu. According to the old legend, Bandau derived from the Rungus dialect. It means the leader of the beast. It was found at the Bandau River by a man named Aki Rungsuid. To protect the town from the British North Borneo, a man by the name of Sharif Usman built a fort at Merudu Bay. The fort was to build to prevent the British from setting up a settlement. Kota Marudu was known for its scenery as the tip of Borneo and the beautiful waterfall at Sorimsin. Kota Marudu has one of the South East Asia largest Solar Power Station. The economic activities derive from oil palm, honey and maize. The maize festival is a regular yearly event.

Kota Merudu District Coordinating Committee

The Kota Marudu District Co-Coordinating Committee was the latest to be formed in the year 2018. The interest shown by the pensioners was overwhelming. The first chairman is Mr Ajmer Singh Gill. As the coordinator in the district, he has to oversee the activities of the pensioners in the district.

The President Datuk Wilfred Lingham addressing the pensioners, during their first inauguration of DCC Kota Merudu 2018

Kota Merudu DCC Committee headed by Mr. Ajmer Singh Gill

Pensioners attending the formation of DCC Kota Merudu 2018

A short depiction of Tongod District

Tongod is a sub-district within Sandakan. Two years after the Second World War, my father Peter Raymond Lai was sent to Tongod. He was to take charge of the dispensary in Tongod. We started our trip from Sandakan cruising along the Kinabatangan River upstream using a small sampan. The trip took us five or more days and had to stop at the river bank for nature call or to prepare meals for the day.

It was an exhausting and grueling journey as we cruised along the Kinabatangan River. The journey was peaceful and calm. Calmness did mean no danger, menacing looking creature called crocodiles were plentiful. Some were seen on the river banks, having the sunbath. Occasionally one or two would emerge and swim close to the boat. The crew was ready with a shotgun if it came to close for comfort.

Besides that, sleeping on a mat laid on hard material and limited space was uncomfortable. Our consolation along the trip was the opportunity to witness the beautiful scenic view and the varieties of animals and birds along the way. Fishes were plentiful all along the river and we had no problem of wild meat.

Tongod District Coordinating Committee.

The Tongod district coordinating committee

PPKS has no plan to set up a district coordinating committee in Tongod. In the year 2017, some pensioners in Tongod heard about the association. They then requested Datuk Wilfred to open up a DCC in the hamlet. It was a personal request and Datuk Wilfred obliged. A group of executive committees went and temporarily set up the DCC.

The committee will make a trip to the town in future to verify its final interest and member's participation. The temporary DCC chairman is Encik Kamidah Bangilon.

A short depiction on the historical aspect of Kuala Penyu district (Turtles)

The district of Kuala Penyu

The population of Kuala Penyu is still insignificant. The beaches were known to be the breeding grounds of sea turtles. The turtles thrived throughout the century. Nowadays turtles can no longer be seen on the beaches. However, the town still maintains its name as Kuala Penyu.

The indigenous tribes that make Kuala Penyu are the Kadazan/Dusun, Bisaya, mixture of Brunei and Chinese.

Moving On

Kuala Penyu old town

During world war two and the Japanese occupation, the people of Kuala Penyu did not suffer much.

One such family that witnessed the Japanese occupation was Mr. Wong Kai Yee. Mr. Wong and his family had to flee to Kampung Bundu near to St Peter's church due to the Japanese harassment.

LUKE WONG KAI YEE @ KAJI (D)
Mr Luke Wong

Mr. Luke Wong had just returned from Hong Kong after attending the LaSalle School. He returned to Kuala Penyu and stayed for a while in Sawangan. Due to his fair complexion, the Japanese mistook him for

Chinese and wanted to kill him. As they were ready to chop his head with their Samurai sword, his mother came running to inform the Japanese that the boy was his son and not a Chinese. He was then directed by the Japanese to climb a tall coconut tree to plug some coconuts. Fearing for his life, he climbed the tall tree much faster and better than a monkey. The Japanese then spared his life.

At the end of the war, the Australian Military force was in Labuan to accept the seal of surrender by the Japanese.

After the seal was signed, the commander of the Japanese Military dispatched signal to all their military garrison throughout North Borneo to lay down their arms. The Allied forces immediately dispatched their combat units and military engineers. They were fully armed and dispatched heavy machinery to the various ports in North Borneo. They landed in Menumbok a coastal town close to Labuan. From Menumbok, they made their way inland using their heavy equipment and military hardware. The local people were amazed at the various heavy vehicles that built the road as they moved forward and towards the coastal town of Kuala Penyu. The army was constructing the road to make way for the main unit to the various designated points to disarm the Japanese soldiers who were in their garrisons waiting for the orders to hand their weapons to the Allied forces.

The military engineers worked throughout, to ensure the road was ready for the other combat units to build their advance base and safe perimeter in the village of Kuala Penyu.

With their garrison fully ready, they began to move inland towards several towns such as Beaufort, Tenom, Keningau, and Papar. The local people called the heavy machinery Lipan as the vehicle plunged right through everything on the way.

A dramatic sight enjoyed and amazed by the village children. When the Australian military set up their headquarters in Kuala Penyu, Mr. Wong Kai Yee who was well versed in English was appointed to look after the military store. A store where essential goods were kept to be distributed to poor villages around the hamlet.

He later married a dusun lass by the name of Rose Mary Manakbt Usai, and had three children. He worked for a while for the British Government but later worked for a rubber company called Japangah rubber estate in Beaufort. When the supervisor Mr G.S. Tuxford left for Australia, Mr.

Wong left the company and worked for the Government as a rubber fund board in Tawau. During the Malaysia and Indonesian confrontation in 1963, he resigned and went back to Kuala Penyu to concentrate on his coconut plantation. He took a short stint as a rela officer in Kuala Penyu till he retired. He died at age 92 in Kota Kinabalu.

The Kuala Penyu DCC

Our president was not aware that some pensioners from the district were keen to set up a district coordinating committee. It was only in 2018 that finally the President agreed to bring the pensioners under one roof in the district itself. This was to provide some activities that pensioners could indulge in, other than their past time of fishing or hope on a ferry to Labuan for Arimiti. There were more than twenty pensioners attended. The President gave a brief introduction to the present issues of PPKS.

A temporary committee was formed. Several pensioners were nominated in the committee. Mr. Innocpent became the first chairman to lead the association in Kuala Penyu.

The Kuala Penyu DCC

The newly formed committee to lead the pensioners in Kuala Penyu

Meeting old friends and getting to know one another

A short depiction on the historical aspect of Labuan district. (Federal territory)

Labuan new township 2018, Malaysia

When I was in the service, I often heard of Labuan, but never put my foot on that piece of the island close to home. I had the chance in 1980 when I was on my way to Kuala Lumpur on a military plane Karibo. After a month of intensive training at the Military training camp in Ipoh, I stayed in the transit officers' mess at Jalan Tambun waiting for the military flight.

I visited an old family friend who was in Sabah in 1963 during the confrontation. I went to the military camp and met Captain Au Yong and went for lunch with him. After staying a week at the officer's mess, I managed to catch a flight on a military plane at the Sungai Besi Military airport. As we were approaching Sabah, I managed to have a glance at an island of Labuan from the air. It was surrounded with beautiful sand that looked like the pearl. We landed at the Labuan airport and user to the officer's mess.

I stayed several days in Labuan and met an old friend Jeffrey Rajaya who was the OCPD on the island. It was Christmas eve and he brought me to a friend's house to celebrate that night. During the party, I met an old man and enquired from him how the name Labuan was derived. He told me the word Labuan came from the Malay word which means the harbor. Later they shortened it and called Labuan. The next day I flew back to Tawau with Colonial Hassim, the military commander in Tawau.

Labuan in the last century

Undeniably, in the eighteen century, James Brooke might have visited Labuan and was attracted by its beauty. He had a vision of trying to emulate the island of Singapore and make it into a British territory. After knowing that the island was controlled by the sultan of Brunei, through an emissary, he contacted the sultan. At the Sultan's palace, he made an agreement to help him in the war against the pirates. The sultan had greatly concerned of piracy along the shore of Borneo. Marauding pirates from Tuaran to the rest of coastal Borneo was a pain in the neck for the Sultan.

James Brooke could have taken over with military might, but he had to do it with the British rule of Law.

He needed to discuss and get the approval of the indigenous tribe or the Sultan.

When James Brooke offered to clear the areas of the menace, the Sultan agreed to sign an agreement to lease out to the British the island of Labuan called the treaty of Labuan.

Before the signing could take place, James Brooke ordered a British Naval Officer Rodney Mundy to visit Brunei with his ship called HMS Iris. A tactic used by western power to intimidate the locals by showing their military might. James Brooke was afraid that the Sultan might retract his agreement. Fearing for the consequences of not keeping his initial agreement, the Sultan of Brunei had no choice but to accept the British offer, especially when the naval frigate was pointing his gun towards the shore where the sultan lived.

Before the signing, James Brooke brought Pangiran Mumin to witness the island accession to the British Crown. It was signed on 24 Dec 1846 and James Brooke was appointed as the first governor of the island. He named the town "the capital of Victoria".

The coal chimney in Labuan, Sabah Malaysia

Coal was found on the island and the first company that started to operate on the island was the Eastern Archipelago company. In 1890 the company could not sustain and sold its interest to the British North Borneo Company.

The railway carrying coal in Labuan Island

The underground tunnel of Labuan Coal Mine

Moving On

The Japanese occupation

During the Second World War, Labuan was occupied by the Japanese and the island was renamed to Maida Island. The occupying force was short lived as the war was not in favor of the Japanese.

Labuan was attack by the Allied forces by air before the final invasion Courtesy of Datuk Wilfred Lingham

The Australian forces landed in Labuan.
Courtesy of Datuk Wilfred Lingham

On 10 June 1945, the allied force began their invasion and landed at Tanjung Putri. It took less than a week for the Japanese to surrender. The British restored the name back to its original name that remained till today. The island was then administered by the British Military Administration

The Australian forces in Labuan 1945 Courtesy of Datuk Wilfred Lingham

It joined the North Borneo Crown Colony on 15 July 1946. The Sabah Government ceded Labuan to the Federal Government in 1984 and became a federal territory. The island was declared as an international offshore financial centre and a free trade zone in 1990.

Labuan has the largest memorial site for all the allied soldiers being killed during the Second World War. Many died during the forced death march from Sandakan to Ranau. After the war, their bodies were found and buried in Labuan.

Moving On

The Labuan District Pensioner Coordinating Committee of Labuan

The Sabah Government Pensioner Association had formed the DCC in most of the large populated areas in the state except Labuan.

In the year 2016, the top guns of the association went to Labuan to find out themselves the possibility of forming the DCC, but the response was lukewarm and not many responded to the call.

Disappointed, we waited for another year and putting out feelers to several retirees on the island.

The President Datuk Wilfred Lingham did not give up and continued to peruse the case.

Finally, on 18 April 2018 another followed up took place. We went to two towns. The first stop was at Kuala Penyu. We managed to galvanize several retirees to form the temporary DCC committee in Kuala Penyu.

In the afternoon we left Kuala Penyu and went to Menumbuk via the Menumbuk ferry.

President of PPKS on the way to Labuan.

The PPKS Committee on their way to Labuan to form the PPKS DCC. From left: Evelyn Lim, (Vice President) Bryan Paul Lay, (Deputy President) David Ho (Treasurer), Datuk Wilfred Lingham (President), Joseph Jominol (Vice President) and Hamid Harun (Secretary General)

The next morning, we had our first meeting. It was well attended and issues raised were fully clarified by the President Datuk Wilfred Lingham.

The attendance at the meeting in Labuan was much improved than our previous visit. After a brief preview of the association by the President, many joined in and the DCC was officially launched.

The Labuan DCC committee led by Puan Siti Mazmah binte Haji Awang Damit.

Puan Siti Mazmah with new DCC committee

The new chair lady, Siti Mazmah binte Haji Awang Damit became the first female DCC. A challenging post for her, but she was confident that she will be able to handle the matter well. PPKS Kota Kinabalu will assist her both morally and financially.

Members of the DCC at the meeting in Labuan

We left Labuan the next day and arrived at Kota Kinabalu at around four in the afternoon relieved at our mission accomplished.

A short historical aspect of Sipitang district (Kerangar)

Sipitang town in the sixties

Sipitang town in the early days. By courtesy of James Ku Hen Leong

A little town which I visited in 1988 with a group of young entrepreneurs from USORA, acronym for United Sabah Overseas Returnees Association. During the visit, we attended a briefing at the Forest Industries paper mill preview on the industry's future prospect. Later during the years, it was taken over by an Indian company called Balarpur Industries Limited.

This little town was known to be the most remote area in the state of Sabah. In the seventies, government servants found impertinent or who did not perform well, would be transferred to Sipitang. These were some of the remakes by some of my colleagues during those days.

However, during my recent visit, I found that Sipitang has much to offer. A sleeping economic giant that was just about to wake up from its slumber. A beautiful town with the temperature slightly cooler than the rest of Sabah except Kundasang.

The present project of the trans-state road linking to various countries in the Borneo state would boost its economic activities. Further to that the proposed oil and gas industrial park, the Sabah Ammonia Plant will have spurred the economic activities of the town.

Two well-known areas are the Long Pasia and Long Mio where we could find some attraction at the Kerangar Park and the Mega waterfall. Both the areas are known to attract many tourists from overseas. The tribes that make the hamlet on the move are the Kedayan, the Lundaya, the Lun Bawang, Muruts and Brunei Malay. This town might one day be the transit point between the various known destinations in the state of Sabah.

The Sabah Pensioner Association has no plan to set up the district coordination committee but would probably consider it in the very near future.

A short note on the historical aspect of Telupid district. (Death march)

I visited this small kampong town in the early seventies, on the way to Kota Kinabalu. We did not stop for any refreshment as they were no proper shop to cater to our needs. Only one small wooden shop available located close to a small bridge on the left side of the road. Both sides of the road were rows of big timber trucks and four wheels drive vehicles.

Telupid town in the fifties

Timber was widely extracted during that era. Telupid was well known in international circles due to the death March events that occurred during the Second World War.

The allied prisoners from the prison camp in Sandakan were forced to trek on foot through jungles, ravine, and hills. Many did not make it due to exhaustion, lack of food and medical supplies. Only a handful survived the trip as they reached Ranau. To commemorate the event, the Australian Government and the Malaysian government jointly built the road infrastructure. As a result of this upgrading facility, Telupid became a sub-district during the USNO government. The inhabitants were mostly the Dusun tribe.

During my recent visit to Sandakan in 2016, I stopped at the coffee shop and had some food. I noticed Telupid has developed greatly during the last few years. More government building, schools and shop houses were built turning the once quiet village into a small busy town.

The once timber boom that spurred the economic activities has now being replaced by oil palm. Government officers who came from other districts on duties have opted to make Telupid their permanent home and develop their plot of land available to them. Telupid as in other small towns in Sabah is experiencing a better future prospect. Most basic facilities such as schools, hospital, health clinic, government offices and shop houses are made available to the populace.

The Sabah Government Pensioner Association has not given any consideration to starting the District Coordination Committee. It would consider if the pensioners in Telupid request for it.

EPISODE 28

Tribute

My stay in Kota Kinabalu has been fulfilling. A complete change of environment, since I left Tawau a decade ago. Once a while I paid a visit to my old hometown. Taking part in events organized by the pensioners.

Out of these many events, the most that reawaken my memory were:

A get-together of great significance as they marked their respect and appreciation to their former teachers of the school. The ultimate events were the party at Emas's hotel where about eighty ex-students attended. The gathering had great noteworthy as students of the past took the initiative to organize an event to rekindle their affection for their former school.

A reunion event or get together by all the Ex-pupils of the St Patrick Primary School since 1982.

A word of thanks to the ex-students of St Patrick Tawau by the former headmaster Bryan Paul Lai

A token of appreciation, presented by one of the old boys Tuan Fadil bin Haji Marsus to the Ex-Headmaster of SRK St Patrick Bryan Paul Lai

At Mas Hotel Tawau Reunion dinner

SRK St Patrick ex-student's reunion at Hotel Emas

Relaxing after a hard day's work by ex-pupils of
SRK St Patrick at the school compound.

Group photo to rekindle their early days as pupils of the school in St Patrick Primary Tawau

The St Patrick 100 Anniversary Celebration held in Tawau, Sabah Malaysia

The old graduation photo at Tawau St.Patrick Secondary School in Dec 12, 1955

The early pioneers of the St Patrick School Tawau

A period to recollect the bitter sweet period of the earlier days.

This was the second event I attended. St Patrick one hundred year's awesome anniversary celebration.

Ex-principals, headmaster, old students and guest were in attendance to share the fruit of achievement. The organizing chairman Dr James Ku and Peter Wong of Hong Seng Company had done a superb job to make the celebration an unforgettable event. An event that has great meaning, as I move on to harvest the memories of yesteryear.

Guest and ex-student from overseas were at the celebration (2017)

At the ceremony, Dr Au Yong and Mrs Au Yong (Former Principal of St Ursula convent Tawau Sabah) took an interest to the two books I wrote: A glance of Tawau in the sixties and The Joy of Life

Datuk Mary Yapp my former golfing friend at St Patrick 100 years anniversary celebration

The organizing chairman Mr. Peter Wong, Dr James Ku and the Organizing Committee.

Moving On

100 St Patrick anniversary celebration held in Tawau Sabah Malaysia

Former teachers at St Patrick 100 year's
anniversary celebration in Tawau

    The third event I attended was held on 21 July at the well-known Prominate Hotel in Tawau. Students of Holy Trinity School as far back as in 1950 were present to search for their long-lost pals, schoolmates and classmates.

It was a low-profile event headed by the Holy Trinity Alumni Association chairman Mr. Chia Siew Boon and his committee. They were expected three hundred participants but far exceeded the numbers. An event of joy, happiness and sadness as many of their previous pals had gone. The former principal Mr. Daniel Lee, Mr. James Ku and the rest of the committee had worked hard to ensure the success of the occasion.

The Alumni Welcome dinner.

Mr. Chia Siew Boon Chairman of the HTS Alumni Tawau

The Alumni Association organizing committee of the Holy Trinity School Tawau, Sabah

The cake cutting ceremony to declare the official event.

The three guys from the old boarding house at Holy Trinity School Tawau in 1957 met in the year 2018: Datuk Clement Jaikul, William Kong Kwang Foo and Bryan Paul Lai (Author)

The participants from overseas and other towns attended this very rare occasion at Prominade Hotel Tawau

Keeping the memory alive to welcome the 96 years of ex-Holy Trinity Students

Some of the early birds of Holy Trinity School Tawau. On extreme left: Mr Vun Kou Pau the artist of Holy Trinity School who designed the first school badge.

After the reunion at Prominade Hotel in Tawau, these girls from Kota Kinabalu took time off to enjoy themselves before returning to Kota Kinabalu

For all time sake.

The time has come to be amongst friends and make life interesting as you move on.

My compliment to the State Library. Mr. Wong Vui Yin the director of the State Library receiving the books

A complimentary book to the district officer of Semporna 2018. Presented by Datuk Wilfred Lingham

Complimentary book to Datuk Peter Thien presented by Datuk Wilfred Lingham President of PPKS Kota Kinabalu

The complimentary book presented to Encik Ansari entitled "Ä GLANCE OF TAWAU IN THE SIXTIES"

Presenting a book to Datuk A.Asrie Hj.A.Kadir(An old pal from Tawau) Hap Seng Holding. Left is Sim Siew Meng from Tawau but now station in Hong Kong as the Financial Director of Lei Shing Hong Limited

Presenting a book to the assistant minister of Agriculture and food industry

Datuk Haji Musbah Haji Jamli

The prime mover of the Sabah Pensioner Association from left: Tan Sri Simon Sipaun, Datuk Wilfred Lingham and Datuk William Gabriel

Meeting the old friend, the house speaker of the Legislative assembly of the state government Datuk Sri Syed Abas Syed Ali in the center and on the left is Datuk Wilfred Lingham

Open house at every important festival is a norm gesture by the state government of the day.

Moving On

Guest and members of MPMS Kota Kinabalu with the Minister of Pembangunan Masyarakat dan Hal Ehwal Pengguna Datuk Hajah Jainab Datuk Seri Panglima Haji Ahmad Ayid in Kota Kinabalu

Tan Sri Simon Sipaun, Datuk Wilfred Lingham, Syed Mohamed idid bin Dato' Syed Ahmad Idid (General Manager of PIDM) members of PPKS and officials from PIDM

Associates of MPMS to thank the chief minister for his allocation to all NGOs in Sabah

Down memory lane, the North Borneo Railway where the author's grandfather was working in 1918

Moving On

Down memory lane train ride from Kepayan to Papar

The Sabah railway is still using steam to run. It is meant for tourists and interested parties.

Bakau logs are used to steam up the engine

The author's family at Kundasang Mount Kinabalu
Sabah, Malaysia. Taken in 2018

Fronting today's world

The good old days had gone. We are now fronting a different world. We have to move with the tide and strive for everything under the sun.

In the past, no fence link or concrete wall necessary to prevent unwelcome guest. Neighbors came with no invitation required. A close society where everyone knew each other. Such situation had long gone and we are now in a world of cautious and wary of everyone we are not familiar with.

Every stranger that we meet could be a possible con-men or a rift raft. The housing estate is well guarded. In the very near future, robots will be used, to cater your need to open your gate or door. Many new challenges are coming as we confront a new world order.

My sincere Dedication

I dedicate this third and final book to my family, children, grandchildren, the Sabah Government Pensioner Association Kota Kinabalu, the Sacred Heart Alpha Group, the Sabah Credit Cooperation Penampang Senior citizen, the twentieth-district coordinating committee of the Sabah Government Pensioner Association and all steadfast friends who gave me the inspiration to begin and to end the final episode of this book "MOVING ON".

Finally, should there be any discrepancies, names wrongly spelt or words written that might inadvertently hurt anyone, do accept my sincere apology.

The author Bryan Paul Lai and Spouse Lilian Koh Lee Kyaw
In Kundasang Ranau Sabah Malaysia
Bryan Paul Lai. PPN ADK
Email: sinontiku@gmail.com

www.ingramcontent.com/pod-product-compliance
Lightning Source LLC
Chambersburg PA
CBHW040107100526
44584CB00029BA/3824